Praise for Erica Spiegelman and

"Get *Rewired*! This phrase has two meanings. The first is get this book if you are interested in increasing your recovery capital. Recovery capital is concerned with the resources you can bring to bear on establishing and maintaining your recovery. *Rewired* will definitely increase your recovery capital. The second meaning to this phrase is that *Rewired* will also help you rewire some of your old or stinking thinking. Einstein has been credited with saying that you can't solve a problem with the thinking that created it. This couldn't be more true for the person suffering from addiction. Recovery requires a 180 degree shift in how you think about yourself, your relationships, and your problems. *Rewired* helps you develop a useful and practical perspective on what you can do to recover from this dreadful condition. I highly recommend this book."

—Allen Berger, Ph.D., author of *12 Stupid Things That Mess Up Recovery, 12 Smart Things to Do When the Booze and Drugs Are Gone*, and *12 Hidden Rewards of Making Amends*

"The *Rewired* approach models the importance of addressing addiction by becoming one's own best guide rather than a follower of someone else's directives. It shows a way of acceptance for an addict as well as friends and families affected by addiction. *Rewired* provides the principles and actions to cultivate and re-enforce a healthy self. It offers the tools to plot a path and to proceed step-by-step toward maintaining positive change. Erica Spiegelman has a strong and steady voice that is certain to inspire those troubled by addiction to feel confident in the path toward recovery that they designed and implemented."

—Gayle Byock, MA/MFT

"There are so many mysteries surrounding addiction that not even the best medical people can solve them. That's why we need a sort of 'addiction detective' to get to the bottom of these horrific diseases. In *Rewired*, our detective is Erica Spiegelman who, in plain, simple language, offers us a path to a better life. As it turns out, we were born with all the tools: love, hope, gratitude, honesty, and compassion. Erica explains how to use what we already have or can attain to navigate not just addiction but all the challenges of life. In the end, like Dorothy in the *Wizard of Oz*, we *can* go back home and we *can* make a difference. One of the best recovery books I've ever read."

—Pat O'Brien, radio host, TV anchor, and author of
I'll Be Back Right After This

"I have worked with Erica Spiegelman for several years in various treatment settings. I often refer clients to Erica and I hold her in the highest professional esteem for a number of reasons. Erica has an amazing ability to connect to people on a deep and sincere level. I consistently receive amazing feedback about her from our shared clients. She takes a holistic approach to treatment, meaning she helps individuals grow healthy spiritually, physically, and emotionally. She challenges her clients to become better people, but she does this in a completely safe and nonjudgmental manner. Her approach is forward thinking and innovative while maintaining a down to earth, intuitive wisdom. As a person, she has a bright loving energy that emanates to those around her."

—Amy Reichenbach, Psy.D., Licensed Psychologist

"I have known Erica Spiegelman for 6 years and I can't say enough good things about her. She is brilliant with clients and colleagues she works with. Erica has a true gift of taking her clients to the next level so they can have the success they much deserve. I have loved to watch her work and grow in our industry."

—Ross Remien, Director and Founder, Living Rebos
Outpatient/Sober Livings

"There are few people who truly understand the disease of addiction and the attainability of recovery as well as Erica Spiegelman. *Rewired* is a must read for anyone seeking the essential internal tools to make recovery a reality."

—Robert L. Shapiro, Attorney and Chairman, The Brent Shapiro Foundation for Alcohol and Drug Awareness

"Erica was my Chemical Dependency counselor while in rehab and while I was in an Intensive Outpatient Program (IOP). She helped guide me through so many tough times, I don't think she knew how often! There are times now that I may be feeling off and I can hear Erica in my head asking if that's best for me. She will always be a dear friend and I thank her so much for helping to guide me through those dark days! Oh and I have been clean from opiates for 18 months!"

—Mary Tercero, client testimonial

"Working with Erica has helped me realize that it was my behaviors that needed to change. She helped me see that I am worthy of change, a good life, and health. I highly recommend seeing Erica for counseling and guidance. She helped change my life. I have stopped using substances and am sober almost two years. I have so much beauty in my life now."

—Jake T., client testimonial

ERICA SPIEGELMAN

REWIRED

A BOLD NEW APPROACH TO ADDICTION AND RECOVERY

hatherleigh
Improve your life. Change your world.

Improve your life. Change your world.

Hatherleigh Press is committed to preserving and protecting the natural resources of the earth. Environmentally responsible and sustainable practices are embraced within the company's mission statement.

Visit us at www.hatherleighpress.com and register online for free offers, discounts, special events, and more.

Library of Congress Cataloging-in-Publication Data is available upon request.
ISBN 978-1-57826-565-7

All Hatherleigh Press titles are available for bulk purchase, special promotions, and premiums. For information about reselling and special purchase opportunities, please call 1-800-528-2550 and ask for the Special Sales Manager.

Interior Design by Cynthia Dunne

20 19 18 17 16 15 14 13 12
Printed in the United States

CONTENTS

To every soul that has been touched by addiction.

ACKNOWLEDGMENTS

My intention by writing this book is to help people; to give them hope and a way to lead and live a healthy life. I am sharing what has helped me and countless others. Every person deserves to find a path to sobriety and a life full of health, happiness, and love. I am here to help you navigate your journey.

This book is for everyone. It's for the sober, newly sober, those who are contemplating getting sober, those who may be dependent on substances, those struggling with unhealthy habits, and for anyone trying to change their life for the better. This book is also intended to help the friends and family of those struggling with addiction.

I would like to thank the people who have shown unconditional support, friendship, companionship, and love.

My mother, Susie, who gave me life, also saved my life. She never gave up. She asked me over and over again if there was something wrong and if I needed help, until I cracked. Thank you, Mom, for your unconditional love; for being so persistent, resilient, comforting, caring, and supportive; and for being my light.

To my Dad, Marc, thank you for being my number one supporter and champion. You have been unconditionally "bursting with pride" in everything I have done in life. You have always made me feel so loved, safe, and special.

To Jayne, my stepmom, for being my biggest cheerleader, always supporting me, and for being a rock for our family—proud, loving and someone who I can talk to about anything. Thank you.

To my wonderful brothers, Max, Jordan, and Joe. Thank you for allowing me to be my authentic self, for always showing me your support and love, and for telling me how proud you are. I am so lucky and grateful to be your sister.

To my other family members—your endless love, wisdom, care, laughter, and support has helped me get to where I am today: Jessica, David, Alex, Olivia, Jean, Sandy, Aaron, Elyse, Carrie, Fred, and Bari.

I would like to acknowledge my grandparents who gave me unconditional love and cared for me from Day 1. Marty Abram (Papa) and Lee Spiegelman (Bopi). To my grandmothers, who are no longer living but will always be with me in spirit. To my Hiya, Ruth Abram and my Nanny, Joy Spiegelman.

To my people, who are in my life and listen to me day in and out, and through the years. You have stuck by me through life's highs and lows, showing me unwavering support, encouragement, and immeasurable love: Xavier, Amy, Alison, Courtney, Erica, Jake, Kourtney, Melissa, Karla, Samantha, Julia, Adam, and Dustin.

To my clients, it has been a privilege knowing and working with you. You have shared with me your stories, struggles, pains, and joys. My life is better because you are in it. Thank you for allowing me to walk beside you and help you on your path. It is, and has been, an honor.

Thank you to all the brilliant peers, therapists, counselors, and friends I have worked with in the recovery world. You know who you are. Your dedication, empathy, commitment, love, and determination to help others is extraordinary! You have been there supporting and encouraging me all the way.

To the people who helped make this book come alive:

Marza, thank you, for all your time and energy. You brought harmony, beauty, and flow to the pages.

To Hatherleigh Press, my publishers, editors, and publishing team: Andrew Flach, Ryan Tumambing, Ryan Kennedy, and Anna Krusinski, I appreciate all the help along the way. Thank you for your guidance and for having faith in me.

I am very grateful to some people I did not mention who have crossed my path and have been part of my journey. In the many chapters of my life, I have encountered some wonderful souls who have taught me many lessons—thank you.

I love you all and having you in my life has enriched it in ways that I will never be able to fully express. Thank you from the depths of my spirit and from the bottom of my heart.

INTRODUCTION

"We must dare to be ourselves, however frightening or strange that self may prove to be."

—May Sarton

The multi-headed serpent of addiction has plagued mankind for centuries, and despite our most brilliant technological advances, the epidemic of substance abuse continues to spread, jeopardizing our futures and those of our children, our families, and our friends. In the last three decades, the number of overdoses has risen by 300 percent; in this year alone, 100 people a day will die from drug-related overdoses. These bleak figures are staggering; however, unlike at any other point in history, we have the chance to reverse our fate.

In the past 20 years, a paradigm shift has occurred—the concept of *recovery* has firmly taken root in our collective consciousness. We now live in an era of great hope—both for our health and for our personal happiness. People from all over the world are starting to discover the joys of physical, emotional, and spiritual self-care. There is a universal hunger for change and enlightenment, and an end to unnecessary misery and suffering.

But this climate of ever-evolving solutions has its challenges. Today, there are practically as many types of recovery programs as there are addicts. Some favor a cookie-cutter approach, churning out an assembly line of sober participants that all follow the same set of rules or regulations; some use religion, "steps," or philosophy to indoctrinate members; some focus exclusively on a physical cure for addiction, while others ignore the body completely and address the emotions. With so

1

many options and directions, it can be difficult to find the "correct" path. Wondering which plan of recovery is right for you can become such a headache that you feel you need a drink just to think about it!

This is where *Rewired* comes in. In this book, we present a simple, common sense approach to recovery that is tailored to the uniqueness of every individual, regardless of his or her beliefs, background, or specific addiction. Each one of us has a distinct physical, mental, emotional, and spiritual make-up. As such, we require and deserve an individualized plan for recovering. You don't need any special knowledge or time in therapy to complete the process. There is no discussion of willpower or "my way or the highway" directives. Through the straightforward process of rewiring the brain, using the new behaviors and habits discussed in this book, thousands have embraced lasting, cellular-level change. This is a path to sobriety that truly works.

The only requirement is that you learn to develop a sense of *Authenticity*—that intuitive inner voice that is so precious and innate to every one of us. Authenticity is what allows us to navigate the challenges of life without compromising our bodies, minds, or spirits. It is the key to long-term freedom from the bondage of harmful, debilitating habits. As you navigate through this book, you will come to explore authenticity in great detail, as well as the related values of honesty, solitude, self-care, gratitude, compassion, and many others. These are the principles that create not only *physical* sobriety, but a mental, emotional, and spiritual sobriety as well—a complete *lifestyle change*, or what I like to call *a whole-soul makeover.*

AUTHENTICITY

The word "authentic" is a combination of Latin and Greek words meaning "coming from the author" and "one who acts independently." I interpret this as, "You are the author of your life." It also means "of undisputed origin" and "accurate; trustworthy; reliable." When your authentic voice can be trusted, there is no need to look elsewhere for guidance. No guru, therapist, teacher, or best-selling writer can give you better answers than the ones you find within. There can be no permanent recovery without an awareness of oneself as unique in all the world. And because no two people will ever think, feel, or live exactly alike, the authentic voice will always be more accurate, more informed to your situation, than any cookie-cutter recovery program. In this way, you can begin to think of recovery as an adventure of deep self-exploration—a journey to your core.

HONESTY

Honesty is the number one requirement for a sober life. There are so many ways that addiction eats away at our instinct to tell the truth—both to others and to ourselves. Over time, lying becomes natural, eroding all trust, intimacy, and personal growth. It creates a life of isolation, insincerity, and estrangement as we become more and more enmeshed in our fantasies and the false reality that addiction creates. Learning to be honest on a daily basis is a life-long process for any addict. In this book, we will present a challenge to be 100 percent honest in our words, actions and emotions for just 24 hours. How do you think you will do?

EVOLUTION

Active addiction is a rut that spawns other ruts in all areas of our lives. This is where the element of evolution comes into play. We have to take a long, hard look at just where exactly we have dropped the ball. Have we quit school or abandoned a cherished dream? Have we neglected our partners, settling into a dead-end pattern of resentment and routine? Have we made do with a life of mediocrity as we secretly wonder what we might have achieved had things gone differently? Our goal will be to catapult you off the couch onto a magic carpet of spontaneity and surprise. You may discover recovery is more fun than you imagined! It is what you make it, so make it about reinventing your life for maximum, substance-free joy, pleasure, and excitement.

SOLITUDE

Solitude is the soil into which we plant our recovery. Without solitude, our recovery cannot put down roots and bloom. It will always remain shallow and short-lived. Learning to enjoy being alone is a critical task for any recovering addict. Our discussion of solitude will explore some of the resistance we face as we try to carve out time for ourselves. It also catalogs some key characteristics of withdrawal from 24/7 dependence on technology. We learn to travel inward, to validate ourselves from within the bejeweled recesses of our own soul, and to cultivate a connection with the natural world. Visualization, meditation, and silence become our allies in a life free from drama and chaos. We begin to value our own company, nurturing our uniqueness and ultimately falling in love with ourselves—often for the first time.

TIME MANAGEMENT

One of the greatest challenges you will face as a recovering addict is the management of your most valuable resource: time. How you spend your time reflects your values, your desires, your hopes and dreams, and the importance that you place on your sobriety. But time management is *not* an innate skill; for many of us, we need outside help to organize our lives in a way that best serves our higher purposes. Oftentimes we don't realize the sheer number of hours we lose to television, the Internet, or gossip. Procrastination and chronic lateness can trigger us to act out through our addiction, rather than face our underlying fears about moving forward in life. As we start learning to set boundaries and to live in balance, we move closer to our goal of rewiring our brains for new behaviors and becoming our own allies in recovery.

SELF-CARE

Despite the best intentions of our caregivers, many of us on the recovery path did not learn how to take care of ourselves as children. As adults, we neglect our bodies, depriving them of nutritious food, sleep, and exercise. We neglect our minds by depriving them of intellectual stimulation and knowledge. Our souls suffer from a lack of attention and respect. In our discussion of self-care, we will address all the different types of self-care that recovery requires. We learn when to say yes, and when to say no. We learn to anticipate dangerous relapse signals long before they become a problem for us. By putting ourselves first, we begin to accept the fact that we are only human. As we come to a deeper understanding of our own limits, we can finally let go of the unhealthy expectations that drive our addictions.

HEALTHY RELATIONSHIPS

Once we have begun to establish a strong, stable relationship with ourselves, it is time to examine our relationships with others. Learning to live in harmony with the people around us requires an attitude of humility, respect, and tolerance, none of which come easily to most of us. We struggle with the desire to control and manipulate others; at other times we give up and withdraw from the world. As we discuss healthy relationships, we will explore the need to separate from unhealthy partners and toxic family members, as well as the need for developing allies and role models. Along with learning to detach with love, building trust is an all-important concept.

GRATITUDE

In studies regarding the rate of survival in cancer patients, researchers found that the single most significant emotion in promoting recovery was gratitude. Those patients who found a way to be grateful for their lives had the highest chance of beating the life-threatening disease. And so it goes for us as addicts. When we live in negativity, entitlement, and anger, we create a vortex of dark energy that only serves to pull us further down into the hole of our addiction. Learning to appreciate all that we are given in this life is essential for our healing. Even if it doesn't come naturally, we must push ourselves toward taking note of life's abundance. Gradually, we will start to feel it in our hearts, as we learn to enjoy giving back to others more than taking from them. We see what we can offer to the world, and how we can repay those who have helped us over the years.

COMPASSION

As with any tremendous undertaking or journey, one needs to cultivate kindness, forgiveness, and a sense of compassion for all the mistakes we have made and will make as we continue on our paths. At the end of the day, our recovery must be based not on shame or perfectionism or the need to impress others, but on our willingness to be kind to ourselves. After all, sobriety is really a gentler, more loving way to live. We must do it out of compassion, and hold compassion as our highest value in dealing with other addicts, strangers, acquaintances, and loved ones. As we let go of grudges, vendettas, and petty hang-ups, it becomes easier to live without our drug of choice. We simply don't need the crutch anymore, as our hearts are brimming with good will toward ourselves and others.

LOVE

Love is the vital energy that makes up our life force. Its invisible rays connect every living thing on this earth, and its healing powers are immeasurable. Love is the culmination of all the other core elements, serving as both their destination and their result. Oftentimes there are negative experiences from our youth that have blocked off the flow of love in our lives, and indeed, our addiction may be masking these injuries. With the help of this book, you will be able to heal the damage at its source, restoring the bountiful, rushing river of love that is your birthright. It can be scary to open up to love after so much pain and struggle, but unless we learn to let love in, we will always be crouching in the shadows, rather than frolicking in the sunlight. As we shall learn, to love is the ultimate human freedom, and the greatest joy we can experience.

As you read through the 10 elements of recovery in this book, remember that no two people will create the same recovery plan. There exists a "continuum of trauma," and each addict will fall somewhere slightly different on the spectrum, according to his or her personal experiences. But whether mild or extreme, no trauma should be considered negligible; no one's suffering should be minimized. Some of us have endured physical, mental, verbal, or emotional abuse in our homes, at school, or at work; others have created the trauma themselves while caught up in the eye of addiction. We've said things we don't mean, engaged in brawls, gotten ourselves arrested, or ended up in car accidents, sometimes walking away without any memory of these events. Some of us grew up with tons of love and had a great support system, yet still fell into an environment where substance abuse was a commonality. A genetic component may also play a role in our addiction. If family members suffered from substance abuse, the odds that we will follow in their footsteps are high. In this way, each recovering person's circumstances and needs will be different. Some may need to focus more heavily on honesty and compassion, while others will need to work harder on cultivating serenity and healthy relationships.

Regardless of where you fall on the spectrum, you will learn to form healthy habits and routines, develop coping strategies, let go of stagnant, negative relationships, open up to new passions and life purposes, embrace the love that surrounds you, and experience sober life as something to celebrate, not just endure. You will learn to self-sooth in the face of all of life's obstacles, relying on your own inner strength and fortitude rather than on a substance, person, or damaging behavior. You will learn to ground yourself in the present moment, which is forever a source of sanity and reliability.

Each chapter in this book contains a story from my own life of addiction, as well as a case study from my practice involving one of these core principles. Using the combination of these two elements, I hope to offer an experience of identification and connection beyond the clinical. Identifying with others and their recovery experience is vital to moving out of isolation and into action. You may not see or hear yourself in every personal story, but you will surely find one or two behaviors or emotions that you can relate to. Try to find common ground in these tales, rather than dwelling on specifics that don't match. Ask yourself, if you exchanged the addiction and perhaps the order of events, would you not recognize yourself just a tiny bit?

To aid in the exploration process, each chapter comes with a brief set of questions at the end. These are designed to help deepen your understanding of the principles and personalize them for use in your own recovery. What is the point of understanding something intellectually if you can't understand it in terms of your own everyday, tactile experience? Answering these questions is also a good way to develop the habit of journaling. Journaling is like turning a spotlight on the unconscious. It brings to the surface many ideas, feelings, dreams, and regrets that we often didn't know existed. It's a type of archaeology in which we seek to uncover our authentic selves. Even if you hate writing, give it a shot; you can even jot down your thoughts in bullet points, if you prefer. However you do it, journaling shows a commitment to this process and to your long-term recovery.

To use this book to its full advantage, you will need to set aside time each day to read, write, and digest the concepts as you go along. This "me" time is non-negotiable. It is the chrysalis every addict needs in order to become a sober butterfly. You must fight for this time and space, even if it's just 10 minutes a day. It is the beginning of the authentic, healthy, happy, and whole new you.

Rewired is not just a self-help book. It is also somewhat of an autobiography. My path to a life of sobriety and authenticity began many years ago, when I was just 25. I was floundering in the deadly waters of alcohol addiction. I found myself spiritless, dangerously close to drowning in a sea of loneliness, desperation and depression. Addiction had deprived me of my interests, my dreams, and my desire to grow. It had stolen the very essence of my being. Instead of friends and lovers, wine had become my constant companion. Drinking made me feel safe and at ease; it helped me to function. I remember being up in bed at night, asking myself, "What happened to me? Where have I gone? What is this empty life I'm living?"

Things had reached the point where I couldn't hold a conversation without getting shaky inside. I could no longer envision a future without alcohol in the picture. I imagined my wedding day; my handsome, charming groom before me, all my friends and relatives watching. Then came the dreaded moment... *How would he ever get the ring on my finger without my hand shaking?* Everyone would see. Everyone would know I had a problem. But it went deeper than keeping up outward appearances. I wondered, for example, how I would ever be able to get through nine months of a pregnancy without drinking. I stayed up many nights, driven to despair by these thoughts. I realized that I had to either take charge of my life, or face a continuing downward spiral where the only outcome was death.

After months of soul searching, I decided to create my own recovery plan. Somehow I knew that the answers I was seeking were inside me. After all, I could remember a time when things had been different: even though I now felt lost, I could still hear a small, persistent voice inside that insisted on healing. I began writing down the basic core values and principles that I had abandoned while intoxicated. The plan was simple, yet comprehensive. It was based on cultivating a healthy mind, body, and spirit, and as I began to follow it each day, I sensed I was recovering on all levels. I found myself living on a new plane of consciousness. It felt miraculous and exciting, and I wanted nothing more than to share my discoveries with others. This led to the desire to become a counselor, and although I had already graduated with a degree in literature, I now sought out certification from UCLA as a California State Certified Drug and Alcohol Counselor.

Today, I use my experience to motivate and inspire clients from all walks of life at one of the most innovative and renowned drug and alcohol treatment centers in the world. I also work as a consultant, public speaker, and author. I lead workshops, appear as a guest on radio and television shows, and contribute to a variety of blogs and websites, all of which I do with a deep appreciation for my sobriety. I do not take my second chance at life for granted; it is a gift for which I show gratitude on a daily basis.

I have worked with hundreds of students, businessmen and businesswomen, married folks, single folks, retired folks, and many other types of people, all with varying degrees of trauma and different needs when it comes to recovery. Many of my clients have struggled to undo years of negative self-talk and bad habits formed in abusive environments. Many lack basic nurturing skills and the ability to express or tolerate emotions. But all have found a way to let go of their addictions and embrace a new lease on life after incorporating the 10 core principles and the process of rewiring.

Through this book, this same healing blueprint is made available to you. It is my great joy to be able to assist you in creating your own personalized recovery plan for mind, body, and spirit. As you travel this proven path, you will be freed of negative, unhealthy behaviors and discover peace, wholeness, beauty inside and out, and a genuine prosperity of spirit. Once you take the first step forward, nothing can stand in your way.

Let the adventure begin!

Chapter 1

AUTHENTICITY

"Always be a first-rate version of yourself, instead of a second-rate version of somebody else."

—JUDY GARLAND

"Our deepest fear is not that we are inadequate. Our deepest fear is that we are powerful beyond measure. It is our light, not our darkness, that most frightens us. We ask ourselves, 'Who am I to be brilliant, gorgeous, talented, and fabulous?' Actually, who are you not to be?"

—MARIANNE WILLIAMSON

For many addicts and alcoholics, it is necessary to first arrive at a "bottom" before seeking treatment or recovery. Sometimes this bottom is a very public, external event, such as a car crash, a DUI, or an arrest. Perhaps it comes as the loss of a job, a major relationship, or one's circle of friends. These types of wake-up calls, with their flashing red lights, pink slips, and divorce papers are harsh, but in a way, they are also a blessing. Having reached this rock bottom point, we can no longer ignore the effects of our actions. The consequences of our addiction have spread beyond our own bodies and minds, spilling into shared spaces and forcing us to confront the reality that we are out of control.

There are also more internal ways to bottom out. Sometimes the bottom manifests as a moment when the despair of living with an active addiction outweighs all former joy, excitement, or relief that was once gleaned from the substance or behavior. We may not know how to get through a day *without* our drug of choice, but we know for sure we can't get through another day of using.

Real Recovery: Erica

I myself experienced this kind of "silent" bottom. An unbearable darkness had crept into my soul, and like a psychic cancer, it was slowly killing me. I could no longer cope with the discrepancy between my values—what I knew to be right and true in this life—and the way I was living. That quiet, small voice of truth inside me could not be extinguished or destroyed, no matter how hard I tried to drown it out. When I finally realized the futility of fighting my inner voice, I broke down and wept. From that moment on, things became easier as I began to live in harmony with my deepest self, rather than in constant, internal conflict.

The voice of the Authentic Self is a wise and intuitive knowing that resides in all of us like a steady candle flame, guiding the way. It whispers to us in dreams, revealing to us our purpose in life and alerting us when we have done or said something incongruent with our values. It informs our decisions on a moment-to-moment basis—*if* we take the time to consult with it. Throughout this book you will discover that all the other core elements lead back to Authenticity. Principles such as Evolution, Healthy Relationships, and Self-Care all require that our actions, speech, and decisions come from a place of authenticity, rather than by conforming to external prompts.

In order to recover my Authentic Self, I had to retrace my steps back to childhood, when I first learned to muffle my true feelings. I was the eldest, and when my parents got divorced, I shouldered the herculean task of "keeping the family together." I donned a mask I like to call "The Rock." If someone asked how I was doing, my only reply was, "Fine!" I desperately wanted the people around me to be happy, and so I began to place less importance on my own thoughts and emotions, and more on the validation I got from pleasing others. Family members remarked on how loving and caring I was, but no one seemed to notice that I was fast becoming a contortionist, bending over backward and forward to accommodate other people's wishes.

Before long, I began experimenting with ways to take the "edge" off of all that responsibility. I would sneak off and get drunk, feeling justified that I deserved some "comfort" after all that self-sacrifice. Of course, I had to lie to my family about where I was going and whom I was with. Soon, I found myself snared in an endless web of deception that only grew stickier the more I drank.

My life became fragmented. I would wander into random bars in the Tenderloin in San Francisco, so as not to run into anyone I knew. I would go by myself to gay bars on Polk Street because I felt safest drinking with gay men; they were always friendly and ready to chat. I found myself sitting next to chronic alcoholics that had been drinking at the bar for 30 years—they were the only other people I could find that would start drinking at 2 or 3 in the afternoon. I would walk to Ghirardelli Square, a tourist destination, where I felt secure in the thought that no one would recognize me there. I am a fourth generation San Franciscan and the probability of running into someone was high, so I went out of my way to not be seen. But I felt ashamed to be hiding. It was embarrassing and degrading. I began to drift and fragment from the person I used to be. It was a time of deep loneliness, despair, and trauma.

Gradually, I began to resemble a broken mirror, with each shard representing a different interpretation of the truth. I had to keep track of every lie, lest my whole life shatter at my feet. This kind of self-betrayal takes a severe toll on one's energy and will. It's literally like living four or five different lives at once. And the more stressed out one feels, the more one needs to medicate with the addiction, deepening a downward spiral that only gets worse with time.

After I got sober, I learned that my pattern was far from unique. Today in my private practice, around 80 percent of my clients reveal themselves to be lifelong people-pleasers. This may conflict somewhat with the stereotypical rock and roll image of the addict as a raging egomaniac who destroys everyone and everything in his path. But oftentimes an addict is just the opposite: a person who is driven to support and help others, often at great peril to his or her own safety, well being, and health.

The typical addict does not care much for discomfort, and living authentically can be highly uncomfortable. Who cares to tell a cherished partner that you need some space? Who wishes to admit to a new boss that you need a day off? It's easier to brush these needs under the rug, not make waves, maintain the status quo, and then drop by the bar at 5 o'clock to "unwind." In fact, I will go so far as to say that inauthenticity, or insincerity, is a major ingredient in the lubricant that keeps most social and professional institutions running like well-oiled machines. We don't want to burden others with the truth; we tell them what we think they want to hear, and in doing so, we take a step away from our own integrity. Whether we acknowledge it at the time or not, this step away from ourselves *hurts*. It causes us pain, and the pain begs to be medicated.

TAKING OFF THE MASK

I spoke earlier about my own "hero" mask, The Rock. This reflex, of adopting an inauthentic guise to protect oneself, is just one of many disguises and defense mechanisms that may surface in reaction to trauma. Many of these masks are unconscious, and until they are explored and eventually surrendered, the addict will remain at risk of relapse.

Take, for instance, the mask of the "loser." This person may crave the negative attention received for screwing up. "At least I'm being noticed," is a common sentiment. This false persona can become so habitual that it fuses with the personality and becomes impossible to shed without help. The more the "loser" plays his part, the more he confirms and perpetuates a negative identity. It can be very challenging to defy one's accepted role in the family as the "problem child" or at school as the "class clown." But deep down, everyone wants to succeed. Every time this mascot for dysfunction acts out her charade, it causes a rift in the psyche. A small, struggling voice of truth is silenced and annihilated, in favor of a false voice, and the consequences are dire.

Another example is the mask of the "invalid." This person gains validation by being perpetually sick, reaping attention in the form of others' pity, allowing friends and family to prove their valor as caretakers. Manipulation becomes second nature, and with every indulgence, the invalid stifles the genuine pain and isolation that results when we fake our way through life.

Understand that none of these masks are moral failings. They are simply strategies developed under duress that are no longer relevant to our lives. Now, instead of helping us survive, they are ruining our chances at happiness, repelling intimacy and fueling our need to drink and use. This is where we need to rewire our brains to think of authenticity as the most effective and desirable way of getting our needs met.

There is an interesting acting exercise I learned in college that perfectly illustrates the seductive quality of wearing masks. Three players are asked to leave the room while a fourth remains alone. The three collectively decide who the fourth player will "be." Let's say they choose to make their pal a "deaf widow." They re-enter the room and promptly begin to relate to their classmate in the manner chosen, for instance by shouting instead of speaking, and by offering condolences at every turn. The fourth player adjusts, often unconsciously, shifting behaviors to meet his or her peers' expectations. Before long, the player has literally become the deaf widow, walking and talking like a bereaved woman who has to constantly ask others to repeat themselves because of hearing loss.

This is what happens during our addiction. People collectively reflect back to us the inauthentic, masked self we are projecting, and their reactions only serve to further cement a false personality. Before long, we have almost entirely forgotten who we *really* are. We are lost.

Of course, casting off one's masks and living authentically is easier said than done. Oftentimes it will take months or even years for others to learn to accept and appreciate the real you. But as long as you live with integrity and stay true to your inner voice, eventually people will come to respect you in a way they never could while you were acting out. There is something magnetic and unstoppable about a person who lives according to the dictates of the heart, instead of as a slave to society's demands. There is a dignity and simplicity in living authentically that cannot be bought, borrowed, or acquired in any other way except through genuine self-searching and introspection.

Furthermore, a person who lives authentically has nothing to fear. There are no skeletons in the closets, no ticking time bombs waiting to explode. One is no longer plagued by the exhaustion of keeping up appearances. Peace of mind and comfort in one's own skin become the norm. The very contentment the addict sought in the substance becomes a daily reality for the sober man or woman living in joyful authenticity.

CULTIVATING AUTHENTIC RELATIONSHIPS

Once we have made a commitment to live an authentic life, we must go to any length to protect our new freedom. We have to be willing to let go of anyone and anything that does not resonate with our deepest truth. The people you choose to share your journey with can make or break your recovery. If you envelop yourself with positive, loving energy, authenticity will bloom into a strong, secure new identity that can withstand all the pressures of life without collapse. This is also a good opportunity to evaluate our work lives, the people we do business with, our landlords, the schools we send our children to, and even the religious centers we attend. We must ask ourselves, "Do these people and places reflect my most authentic, deeply held values? Is there a certain inappropriate behavior I'm tolerating in order to keep the peace?" It may not seem that important at first, but if a daily, mundane interaction is toxic and we don't address it, over time we run the risk that it will trigger our addiction.

Conversely, sometimes other people are not the issue. We may be surrounded by kind, approving individuals who adore us, but despite this we are severely depressed. Maybe we have chosen a profession that doesn't ignite our passion. Yet, fearful of economic instability, we stay put, refusing to follow our authentic bliss. Inauthenticity can manifest in political beliefs or lack of them, our diets, the way we spend our time and money, or even the kind of movies and books we consume. In every area of life, we can ask ourselves, "Does this choice reflect the real me?"

Transforming into an authentic human being can be every bit as turbulent, surprising, and challenging as getting physically sober. In the same way that sobriety is more than just abstaining from a drink or drug, withdrawal is more than just detoxing. There are some very real withdrawal symptoms that come from changing our behavior. We may feel deep bouts of paranoia, anxiety, and fear. After all, we are "coming out" into the world for the first time as our real selves, and there may be repercussions. Some people may like us better the old way, when we did what we were told, didn't rock the boat, and laughed at jokes we didn't think were funny. If we are not used to standing up for ourselves, we may initially feel that life has become a constant state of conflict. Withdrawal from inauthenticity may even manifest as physical aches and pains, headaches, or head colds. All this brain rewiring can be intense, so do not underestimate the size of the step you are taking! Be gentle and be kind. Remember that there is no other way out but *through*.

Although you may feel the world has been turned upside down, there *are* some concrete ways to ground yourself in your new, authentic identity. You can strengthen that inner voice just like a regular muscle through exercise. Journaling, connecting with nature, meditation, and solitude are all excellent ways to amplify your intuition. And like any other new skill, practice makes perfect. It can be helpful to keep a notebook next to your bed at night and jot down any times during the day when you felt disconnected from your true nature. By doing this, you can begin to isolate certain features of your struggle. Perhaps you find that you are outspoken, firm, and confident at your job, but when it comes to dating, you tend to immediately start acting like an imposter. Or maybe you live a 100 percent authentic life—that is, until you step foot into your mother's house, where you instantly contort into someone unrecognizable. All this is great information that can really help you to move forward. You can also use the questions at the end of this chapter as a guide.

Lastly, never forget the value in rewarding yourself for your efforts. You have taken a huge first step toward a beautiful, lasting recovery, and you deserve to be recognized. Just for today, do one kind, healthy thing for yourself!

Questions for Exploration: **AUTHENTICITY**

- In what areas of my life do I lack authenticity?
- In what ways am I a people-pleaser?
- In what circumstances have I ignored my inner voice? Why?
- What are the consequences of ignoring my inner voice?
- In what ways have I betrayed myself?
- What masks do I wear?
- Who are the people who support my authentic self?
- Who are the people who undermine my growth and recovery?
- What is my life's purpose? Am I fulfilling my destiny or hiding from my dreams?
- What changes have I noticed since beginning this work?
- Have I experienced any signs of withdrawal from inauthenticity?
- What have I done this week to strengthen my inner voice? What were the results?
- How did I reward myself this week?

Chapter 2

HONESTY

"Honesty is the first chapter of the book wisdom."
—THOMAS JEFFERSON

Like the arteries that enable the human cardiovascular system, the daily practice of authenticity, integrity, and honesty creates a soul-sustaining circuitry, connecting us to those around us and to our highest selves. Truthfulness flows from our hearts to our minds, manifesting as our words and deeds. Actions such as keeping our promises, refraining from stealing and cheating, and admitting when we've made mistakes all support the longevity, health, and fitness of our spirits. When we are dishonest, even partially, it acts as a kind of blood clot in our soul's flow, blocking energy, threatening our well being, and throwing our lives into chaos.

CAUGHT IN A WEB OF LIES

Lies multiply quickly. Each one acts as an incubator for the next, and before long you'll find you have a real infestation on your hands. An alcoholic may wish to avoid drinking at work, in the car, or during family gatherings, but the relentless physical need to quell the cravings is no match for his good intentions. Eventually he succumbs and must hide the evidence of his addiction in the filing cabinets or the glove compartment. He tells the cop who pulls him over that he "hasn't had a sip all day." His spouse questions why he's suddenly in such a glorious mood, so he invents a phony promotion to explain his booze-fueled euphoria.

As the lies accumulate, they must become more elaborately layered and sophisticated, or else collapse altogether. Now this man must leave home an hour early each day to justify the phony promotion. He has to take a longer, more convoluted road to work to avoid the cop who's grown suspicious. He has created a world of 24/7 fiction that constantly threatens to implode, tumbling down on his head like a load of bricks. In an effort to combat the enormous pressure, he once again turns to alcohol, forgetting that his drinking is the very thing that got him into such a mess in the first place.

This story may sound extreme or even comical, but take note that dishonesty always starts casually. Most of us are merely trying to preserve a sense of stability in an often tumultuous world. If we come from trauma, the need to maintain a fantasy life can compel us to forsake all common sense. The portrait of an addict caught in this desperate cycle of misguided self-preservation is heartbreaking, for as senseless and reckless as his or her lies may seem on the surface, the underlying pain, alienation, and confusion can be all too familiar.

In my own life, I was often very dishonest with my mother. I was so ashamed of my drinking that I would lie to her about where I was and what I was doing. I wouldn't meet her for lunch because my hands were shaking, and she began to notice those physical signs of addiction. She confronted me several times, and I denied I had a problem. I attributed the shakiness to coffee.

The need to hide a substance abuse problem is just one reason for dishonest living. There are dozens more. Shame can be a powerful influence, coursing through our veins like electricity and setting off a chain reaction of spontaneous lies. When we are made to feel embarrassed, inferior, or incompetent by our peers or authority figures, shame can cripple our ability to tell the truth, turning us into spastic, reactionary creatures whose only goal is to avoid further humiliation. In this situation, healing only comes when we grieve the initial trauma, accepting others and ourselves as imperfect. Slowly we can begin to believe that we are loveable as we are, flaws included. The need to impress is gradually replaced with the thrill of being embraced as a fallible human being.

Yet another reason people lie is to control and manipulate others. Often a person who has been traumatized by bullying or domination will feel weak and helpless. This in turn creates a need to strike preemptively, gaining the upper hand in every situation. The control freak lives in constant fear of annihilation, so she goes on the offensive, becoming the very power-hungry predator from whom she once hid. But healing can only occur when this person is willing to touch the center of his or her own sorrow, sit down with the primal feelings of terror and hopelessness, and surrender their need to hurt others. By taking responsibility for his or her actions, this person can finally be free of these self-sabotaging behaviors.

Many times when I discuss honesty with my clients, they will bring up the subject of "white lies." These are the subtle, seemingly harmless untruths that we all tell in the name of diplomacy, politeness, convenience, or habit. Sometimes we tell white lies to score points with our partners, to get a job, or to cover up a mistake. We justify our actions, putting these false words on a special shelf where they can't be classified as truly damaging.

Nonetheless, there are consequences for every lie, no matter how "harmless." These minor fibs contribute to a lack of intimacy; they erode our friendships, work relationships and romantic partnerships. People sense we are putting up a wall and they feel pushed away, even if they don't consciously perceive our dishonesty. Each white lie is another brick in our fortress of isolation, from which we can safely operate without ever having to risk vulnerability.

Lying of *any* kind lowers our self-esteem. We are reinforcing our feelings of inadequacy every time we try to make ourselves look and sound just a little bit better than we *think* we are. A truly confident person at peace with himself/herself does not need to reach for this crutch.

Lying brings unnecessary drama into our lives, and for any recovering addict, this is pure poison. I will give you an example from my own experience. I had recently stopped drinking, and considered myself to be living a decent, mostly authentic life. Sure, I still told a few baby whoppers here and there, but who didn't? I shrugged off the notion that I was doing anything wrong. One day, a friend of mine invited me to a birthday party. I didn't want to go, so I lied by saying I had to be somewhere with my brother. No sooner did these words escape my lips, than I suddenly remembered that my friend lived in the same neighborhood as my brother—in fact, her house was just blocks from his apartment!

Instantly, I was plunged into a state of torture, terrified that my friend would run into my brother at the supermarket, or see him hanging out alone in a coffee shop. At this point, I had to laugh. Why had I bothered to lie in the first place? I had taken whatever brief discomfort and awkwardness the truth might have caused and replaced it with hours of racing thoughts, guilt, shame, and regret. It was at that moment that I said, "Enough!" Living honestly is living honestly—period. Either something is a lie or it isn't. There is no gray area. To be truly sober and *stay* sober, one must always be honest.

Let's talk for a moment about lies of omission. These range from failing to correct someone when they make a false statement about you, to more serious offenses, like failing to declare cash income to the IRS. Even keeping a secret may count as a lie of omission, if it would cause others great harm, were it to get out. This type of lying can be harder to give up, because it involves stepping forward to speak the truth rather than refraining from speaking lies. Omitters will sometimes feel justified in their deception, believing that as long as they didn't utter false words, they can avoid the consequences of an actual lie. But the deceit of secrecy is just as hurtful as outright dishonesty.

Real Recovery: James

To illustrate, consider the following story about one of my clients, a man named James. He was a husband and father who for many years had been hiding his homosexuality from his wife, co-workers, family, and friends. No one thought to ask him if he was living a double life, so he just omitted that part of his experience from every conversation. Throughout his marriage to Sara, whom he considered his best friend, James not only kept his secret but felt deeply ashamed that he was gay. He buried his pain and developed a cocaine habit that was fueled by affairs with men. His drug use helped him forget about the secrets and lies, for a time; but predictably, Sara finally found out that he wasn't the man she had agreed to marry. Both their marriage and their friendship ended, and James realized that concealing his real identity had caused him and those he loved a great deal of pain. James' recovery plan focused on being honest with his family, his friends, and his coworkers. Once he felt safe and courageous enough to begin living his truth, he could finally move forward and treat his drug addiction.

LYING TO OURSELVES

So far we have primarily been discussing the consequences of lying to others. But our relationship with ourselves suffers equally, if not more so, from a continuous refusal to live with the truth. Denial steps in to erect its iron curtain, veiling our every attempt to take a genuine look at our past, present, and future. We minimize the effects of our addiction, make excuses, or exaggerate another's drinking to avoid looking at our own.

We use a bad day to globalize and declare our entire life a failure, and then we comfort ourselves with our drug of choice. We take a moment of poor judgment and turn it into a catastrophe, blowing our faults out of proportion and once more seeking solace in a bottle or a pill. All these forms of dishonesty need to be addressed if we are to live sober one day at a time. We have to call a spade a spade.

Conversely, we can no longer afford to lie about our assets, either. We must begin to acknowledge our abilities and strengths and consider disowning them as an act of self-treason. When we commit to honesty, we don't get to hide the good in us any more than the bad. Every human being is a mixed bag, and as we come to accept both our warts and our beauty marks, we can finally let go of the drain that dishonesty places on us, as it steals away our confidence and our strength, leaving nothing in return.

TURNING THE TIDES

The good news in all of this is that, regardless of its origin or flavor, the insidious lying habit can be permanently reversed with a single, courageous moment of truth. The human spirit, much like the human body, is remarkably resilient and robust. Even a man or woman whose every word has been a lie for decades can wake up one morning, decide to start being honest, and immediately be vaulted onto a plane of existence that he/she never imagined was possible.

The act of telling the truth is like an instant relief serum, a neurochemical tonic that restores ease, pleasure, and a sense of peace. This truth serum works faster to elevate your mood than any street drug, supplement, or pharmaceutical on the market. Our brains are highly adaptable computers that can be "reset" and reprogrammed to live each day in a state of comprehensive integrity. If we can visualize our chronic dishonesty as a broken microchip that we can remove and throw away, we can avoid attaching too much morality or pathology to our lifestyle change and simply embark on a new adventure in truthfulness starting *right now*. One of my old friends coined a great saying that always cheers me up when I'm feeling discouraged: "It's a *new* minute!"

Today I will present you with a special challenge. Are you ready? I dare you to go an entire 24-hour period without uttering a single lie. You must be 100 percent truthful in your actions, words, and emotions for one whole day. Do you think you will succeed? Write down what you experience. Does your body resist with aches and pains, headaches, or skin allergies? Or do you experience a feeling of levity and tranquility? Try to see yourself as a scientist/explorer in unfamiliar terrain, faithfully recording your journey in your "captain's log." Remember that no harm can ever come from knowing, speaking, or living your truth. You may experience setbacks, a loss of fair-weather friends, and even political opposition in extreme cases, but ultimately you will finally be free—free from mental, emotional, physical, and spiritual bondage to addiction and a life of lies.

As cheesy as it sounds, honesty truly is the best policy!

Questions for Exploration: HONESTY

- How have I lied to hide my addiction?
- Have I engaged in cheating or stealing during my addiction?
- What white lies do I tell and why?
- What lies of omission do I tell and why?
- What role has shame played in my dishonesty?
- What role has manipulation and control played in my dishonesty?
- Do I lie to keep others at arm's length?
- How has dishonesty undermined my personal relationships?
- With family?
- With friends?
- With romantic partners?
- How has dishonesty undermined my professional life?
- In what areas of my life do I minimize the truth or make excuses?
- In what areas of my life do I exaggerate the truth?
- Do I distort the truth about my life through globalization or catastrophizing?
- Is there anything that I am currently in denial about?
- Do I have any traumas or uncomfortable truths about the past that I am not facing?
- Am I hiding my assets, skills, or strengths out of fear, shame, or self-loathing?
- How successful was I at the 24-hour honesty challenge?

Chapter 3

EVOLUTION

"Unless you try to do something beyond what you have already mastered, you will never grow."

—RALPH WALDO EMERSON

"Passion is a feeling that tells you: this is the right thing to do. Nothing can stand in my way. It doesn't matter what anyone else says. This feeling is so good that it cannot be ignored. I'm going to follow my bliss and act upon this glorious sensation of joy."

—WAYNE W. DYER

Every living thing on this Earth is evolving; sometimes slowly, sometimes quickly. They develop, mature, and transform without questioning the process—they simply fulfill their biological destiny, continuing the life cycle and perpetuating their species. Man, however, is unique among organisms; he is both blessed and burdened by his intellect. He is prey to a thousand existential fears: fear of failure, fear of success, fear of mediocrity, fear of the unknown. He is deeply prone to paralysis, crippled by his enormous imagination, the very power that sets him apart from the rest of the beasts. To medicate his achingly self-aware brain as it contemplates this universe and his place within it, he turns to myriad intoxicants and coping behaviors. Through active addiction, man interrupts his own growth, withdrawing from the world and refusing to move forward. This experience of being "stuck in a rut" is a painful one, as it goes against our basic nature to expand. When we are stagnant, we are at war with our own nature.

Being enslaved to an addiction is almost like being frozen in time. We repeat the same dead-end activities day after day as though in a trance. We sense that we are squandering our potential, and secretly we know that we are hiding from life, but our rut is safe and cozy; that's why they call it a "comfort zone." With every passing moment, we mourn the fact that there was something better we meant to be doing with our time—we just can't remember what it was anymore. Keeping things the same becomes a full time preoccupation as we struggle to "maintain." We shudder at the idea of change, yet we soon realize that we can never stay sober without it.

Addiction is like a bargain with the devil. Perhaps we only meant to trade him a few hours of our day for a shot of peace and happiness, but those few hours turn into weeks, years, and decades. We may use that shot to deal with a finite wound from the past, intending only to numb our pain so that we can continue to function, but in turn we create a Pandora's box of new problems while indefinitely neglecting to address the original emotional injuries. In this way we drag out the healing process. Through addiction, we may spend 20 years in avoidance of a trauma that might take only a few years to process and integrate.

Sometimes our drinking and using is simply a crutch to deal with boredom. We crave excitement, adventure, and thrills, but having no idea how to experience those things sober, we return to what we know. We just accept that "having fun" must have negative physical, emotional, and spiritual consequences.

Fear of success and fear of failure are also leading motivators for our stagnation. The question, "What if...?" consumes us, eating away at our every attempt to manifest the careers, relationships, and hobbies that we desire. We are afraid we are too old, too young, too gay, too straight, too fat, too thin, too poor, or too ugly to achieve our dreams, so we drink, use, and hide out, then drink and use more to comfort the loss of our passion. We are angry and discontent, even to the point of lashing out at those around us. Otherwise we are depressed and listless, shirking responsibility for our happiness by assuming we already know the future.

When I was actively involved in my drinking, I felt stunted and spiritually stuck. I felt like my spirit was shrinking. I so wanted to grow, to have the family, job, and partner I had always dreamed of. I also wanted to evolve out of the black hole of addiction. It was in the last three years of my drinking that I began to feel my passions slipping away. The things that had once fulfilled me and brought me joy—music, writing, reading, socializing, being with family, and being physically active— all slowly walked out the door, one by one. Now my only desire was to drink. When you develop an addiction, your personality becomes warped as you slowly adapt to the behaviors that being an addict entails. You have to lie, keep secrets, control your environment. Soon you don't even recognize yourself. The obsession with the substance overrides all desire to move forward and grow. It keeps you stuck, repeating behaviors that do not reflect your true self.

FINDING PURPOSE THROUGH PROCESS

So just how shall we begin to embrace the growth process and gain the courage to change our lives? I fully believe that each one of us has a purpose in life, and finding that purpose is a marvelous adventure that can begin at any age, in any location, under any circumstance. We can rewire our brains to see both success and failure as part of a process rather than as final verdicts about our self-worth. As a culture, we are not always comfortable with the idea of a "process." Appearances and results seem to matter more than the journey. Instant gratification is the law of the land. We pay hundreds of dollars to take shortcuts in every area of life, from get-rich-quick schemes to diet pills. We try to skip the work it takes to get to know someone, jumping into relationships before building a foundation of friendship and trust. When we don't get what we want, we are filled with frustration and turn to our drug of choice.

Processes are messy and require investment, but if every caterpillar regarded his process as too sticky, time-consuming, and ugly to deal with, there would be no butterflies, and therefore far less beauty in this world. We have to learn how to go through a process without judging ourselves, accepting our growing pains as normal and healthy as we take steps toward our destinies.

Oftentimes when an addict gets sober, they will need to begin a process of growth and development. Starting from the point at which they started drinking or using, regardless of whether they did so to cope with trauma or simply for kicks, recovery begins with confronting the original cause. For instance, if someone started drinking at age 13, when they finally stop at age 32, they may find themselves dealing with the emotions and struggles of a preteen. All the feelings they've tried to avoid and numb away are still right there, waiting for them. Addiction and avoidance can work like a cryogenics lab, where all our emotions remain on ice until we are willing to face them.

Growing up as an adult can be a daunting task. It is not for the faint of heart. It's embarrassing, awkward, and filled with surprises, but the only cure for arrested development is development. If we want to be sober, self-evolution is our only path. Luckily, growing up late can also be a lot of fun. We can reclaim all the hobbies and passions we never got to explore as kids. We can also reclaim the natural innocence, optimism, and joy that come so easily to youth. We can experience our sexuality in a new, spontaneous way we never expected. We can upgrade all the wires in our brain with new, state-of-the-art equipment chosen from the wide spectrum of thinking styles we are learning in recovery.

Fear of failure is probably one of the main reasons why we prefer to numb ourselves through addiction rather than move forward. Sometimes we are so afraid of letting others down or disappointing them that their opinions dominate us to the point of paralysis. Other times it is a deep-seated feeling of unworthiness that makes us question our abilities. No one wants to fail, but as I mentioned earlier, there is simply no other way to succeed other than to fail many times. If you know and understand this concept, failure loses some of its sting. It becomes a valuable and necessary learning experience, if only to learn the principle of patience.

The world is filled with examples of people who refused to give up, despite multiple failures. Thomas Edison invented over a thousand light bulbs that didn't shine before he finally made one that did. He once remarked, "I have not failed. I've just found 10,000 ways that won't work." Steven Spielberg was rejected by the prestigious USC film school twice, but he remained undeterred and became one of the most respected filmmakers of his generation. There are many others; it's a powerful tool to jump on Google and begin researching what can be done in life. You will find that for every dream imaginable, there is someone out there who has achieved it and who can give you hope of doing the same. Think you are too old? Search for "late bloomers," and you will be shocked at the results. Actor Samuel L. Jackson didn't achieve success until he was 45, while Oscar Swahn of Sweden won a gold medal in the Olympics at age 64 and a silver medal at age 72!

Seeking out positive role models who reflect your unique circumstances is essential—we all need people to look up to. Without mentors, be they celebrities or ordinary heroes from our lives, we will not gain the perspective we need to overcome all the obstacles in our path. Furthermore, there are organizations, such as SCORE (Service Corps of Retired Executives) or Women in Film, that offer free mentoring to those who want to start new careers. The support is out there—you need only ask for it. Often, fear of failure can be ameliorated by just moving out of isolation and into reality, knowing that when we take one step toward our dreams, the universe takes a giant leap with us in that direction.

These statements can be applied to personal relationships as well. No one enjoys being rejected unless they are a robot or a masochist. It hurts. But the only sure way to wind up alone is to let one or two bad experiences keep you from ever dating again. I have an older friend who is happily married and I was surprised to learn that she had been through at least five recent relationships that didn't work out prior to meeting the love of her life. She simply didn't give up, even after failing five times in a row. To her it was worth it to keep searching and believing that she would find the right person.

I know a man who, while not traditionally attractive, is always dating. His strategy was to challenge himself to ask out 100 women in three months. It became a game to see if he could achieve his goal. Every time he got rejected, he smiled because he knew he was winning. Eventually, a woman (#38 or #39) said yes, and he began a relationship. By then he had become so focused on taking action, that he completely forgot his initial fears.

For those of us with a lot of trauma, personal relationships can be very difficult. But nothing will help us more than a sense of playfulness and adventure when it comes to navigating our love lives. We might be rejected if we put ourselves out there, but at the same time, we are doing something that makes us more alive and more human, and that in itself is a reward worth experiencing.

COMBATING THE INNER CRITIC

Negative self-talk, or what some call the voice of the "inner critic," is the fear of failure's chief handmaiden. This can be the voice of someone from childhood who was always disapproving of us, or it could be an embodiment of our own fears that speaks to us as the voice of "common

sense." Regardless, we need concrete weapons to fight this internal mon-
ster that constantly puts us down. A few tools come to mind. The first
is a bit comical, but I find it works for some people. When I hear my
inner critic chattering, I will pause and firmly say out loud, "No," just
like I would to a puppy that is misbehaving.

Other times, I encourage my clients to repeat positive affirmations
to themselves in the mirror. It sounds incredibly cheesy, but perhaps it's
time to embrace the wonderful cheesiness of self-love! Stand in front of
the mirror and tell yourself, "I love you. You did a great job today." Can
you do it?

Lastly, it's sometimes necessary to do a daily written inventory of
everything you are doing right. Do this for 30 days and your entire
mental outlook will radically change. You will begin to focus on your
assets rather than your flaws; and, in doing so, you will gain a whole new
level of compassion and understanding for yourself. Self-hatred affects
every addict, so we must dedicate ourselves to establishing a policy of
tolerance and kindness within our own thoughts if we want to make
sobriety a long-term way of life.

Real Recovery: Matt

A young man named Matt came to see me. He described himself as
being stuck in a rut and wanted my advice. Being frozen in fear was
a feeling he had lived with since childhood. He had always struggled
with learning disabilities, and these contributed to his low self-esteem
and reluctance to take on new challenges. Now in his late twenties,
Matt was so afraid of change that he couldn't take a chance at a new
job opportunity that had presented itself. Instead, he was smoking
marijuana daily, had little motivation, and seemed trapped in an
unhappy, stagnant life.

Matt's recovery plan focused on self-evolution, empowering him
so that he could break free from his stultifying pattern and try new

things. We explored why he was so fearful of change, and Matt realized that he had a fear of failing. Visualization therapy helped him to see that if he failed at something he was trying for the first time, there would be a lesson that would benefit him next time. Evolving was difficult for Matt because he had never been given the permission to try, fail, or change. No one ever bothered to tell him that he was loveable no matter what. But once he committed himself to moving beyond his rut and exploring the unfamiliar, he was no longer interested in sitting around smoking marijuana, waiting for life to come to him. He was now going out to face life head on.

It may seem strange, but fear of success can be just as devastating as fear of failure. Fear of success often comes into play when a child is more gifted than those around him/her. Unhealthy parents, teachers, and peers react to a talented child with indignation. "Who does she think she is?" They view the child as competition, seeking to "put her in her place." A bright young boy is called "disruptive" because he raises his hand too often in class. A particularly kinetic girl is labeled as having ADD, rather than encouraged to pursue activities like dance or sports that would make use of her frantic exuberance. Another young man is told to stop singing in the choir because it makes him look like a sissy and he's embarrassing his father.

In a hundred different ways, we have been suppressed, repressed, and crushed just for being ourselves. It's no wonder that we fear the consequences of our own skills and powers. It's terrifying to feel that if we surpass our friends, family, classmates, or coworkers that we will be abandoned. It's easier to just drink, not rock the boat, and make sure no one feels insecure around us. The phrase, "It's lonely at the top" haunts us. We would rather be "normal," whatever that means. Unfortunately, in order to be "normal" we have to stuff down our desires and passions with addiction. And we can never stop, for if we do, the pain of betraying ourselves becomes unbearable.

Recovering from a fear of success *can* be achieved, however. It's important to remember that the Ugly Ducking had to leave home, go on a long journey, and discover his peers before fully coming into his own. Even a genius like Mozart had Beethoven and Haydn as contemporaries—you will never be all alone, no matter how unique you are. What's important is that you find you own personal pool of like-minded swans and stop trying to be a duck!

Another useful tool for dealing with the fear of success is to employ the principle of generosity. This is a simple concept, but it can be elusive in our society where we are encouraged to live solely for our own gain and celebrity. Living in generosity means that, instead of focusing on whether our stand-up comedy routine is going to make us famous or not, we try to think about the audience members and how they are feeling. So many have struggled through a difficult day at work, are facing financial problems, or are battling an illness. Life is hard, and laughter is a sorely needed medicine. When you think about making people laugh as a service to them, it takes away some of the chatter and replaces it with a healthy feeling of being useful and caring. When we give freely of our talents for the benefit of others, we forget to be obsessed with the outcome of our performance, whether at a job, onstage, or in a relationship. Why should we deprive an audience of beautiful music by refusing to perform? If we are afraid to date, why not think about how happy another person will be to meet us after wading through a sea of Mr. or Ms. Wrongs? Who knows; maybe we are their dream date!

The more we can be generous with our talents, our compliments, our love, our possessions, and our time, the more confidence we will have and the more we will become comfortable with our own success. Giving is the key to receiving the attention, accolades, and respect that we crave. We can visualize ourselves as silkworms, spinning beautiful threads day in and day out without questioning whether we should, or whether we deserve to, or whether people will dislike us for producing such lovely work. It is just who we are. The honeybee industriously creates deliciousness and no one can do anything about it but enjoy it. Regardless of what kind of animal you happen to be, it is safe to be you.

And most likely, the world very much needs your contributions.

SETTING GOALS

Evolving takes courage, but as they say, "It's never too late to be the person you might have been." As with all the other principles, you can begin changing your brain patterns this very day by setting small, attainable goals, achieving them, and celebrating your success. This in turn leads to a surge in dopamine, a happy brain chemical, which you can build on. You can discover a new kind of high that comes from self-actualization.

During my recovery, I took up running as a hobby. My brother encouraged me to run with him. He said to try two blocks, so I did. For years, I had never worked out, instead pouring poisons into my body. I was in no condition to run. I had no idea how I would reach my goal of running a half marathon. I started small, running just 1 mile and getting as many people to congratulate me on it as possible. Then I increased it to 2 miles, then 3. For a while I couldn't get past 3, but a few months later I found I could run 5 miles. I couldn't believe it. More than that, I felt accomplished, and people told me how wonderful it was that I had found a new hobby. They remarked on how happy I looked and seemed, and that positive reinforcement helped me continue to run. Eventually, I ended up being able to run 26.2 miles in the Los Angeles Marathon, something I never thought I could achieve.

Baby steps are key—baby steps, and lots and lots of praise. I never said to myself, "One mile, eh? Anyone can do that. Stop acting like you're special." Instead I constantly repeated, "Great job!" every time I came back from a run, even if it was just a 10-minute run.

Break your dreams down to the smallest possible unit of action that you know you can accomplish. Succeed at your mini-goal and then celebrate. That is the formula for achieving greatness. If you want to win an Oscar, work on a monologue for 10 minutes and then go out and reward yourself with a movie. If your goal is to go back to school, spend 10 minutes online researching different programs and then take a hot bath. The loftiest of ambitions can be pared down to 10-minute daily actions. Writing a novel is writing one page a day for 300 days. It might get done slowly, but it gets done.

To evolve, we must show up for ourselves no matter what. This new, improved relationship with our self is the foundation upon which happy lives of purpose and joy can finally be built.

Questions for Exploration: **EVOLUTION**

- What do you want to change in your life?
- What are some of your personal "ruts?"
- What do you think is holding you back from making that change and evolving to the next level in your life?
- What is your greatest fear regarding moving forward?
- If you could do anything in life and were guaranteed to succeed, what would it be?
- What might you learn about yourself if you take the risk to make a desired change?
- What new doors might open if you make the changes you envision?
- What steps will you take to support your goals?
- Who are your allies who support your dreams?
- Try doing the positive self-inventory for one week. What are the results?
- How will you reward yourself when you make progress?

Chapter 4

SOLITUDE

"Knowing how to be solitary is central to the art of loving. When we can be alone, we can be with others without using them as a means of escape."

—Bell Hooks

"The inward journey is about finding your own full-ness, something that no one else can take away."

—Deepak Chopra

There's an old wives' tale that states, if you want to have a child, first buy a plant. The thinking is that if you can keep a plant alive, you can graduate to owning a puppy. If the puppy survives, you can consider sustaining a human life. Of course, many successful parents lack a green thumb, but the point is that if we cannot even commit to watering a plant, how will we handle the larger, more involved commitments in life?

In recovery, we can think of our new sobriety as a small, green sprout placed in our care. Learning to nurture and nourish ourselves on a daily basis in simple, healthy ways is a practice that builds a strong foundation for all the great things we want to achieve. We must master self-care if we ever hope to be truly useful, happy, and whole. Just as a plant requires adequate water and sunlight, we require adequate rest, nutrition, and exercise. But besides these needs, we also require solitude.

OUR NEED FOR SOLITUDE

Solitude is like the plant's soil—a place to put down our roots and prepare to bloom. Solitude is also the fertile incubator for creativity and original ideas. We gather important nutrients from solitude: serenity, wisdom, self-knowledge, patience, and perspective. It is impossible to grow mentally, emotionally, or spiritually without these vital ingredients, and as we discussed in the last chapter, unless we are evolving, it won't be long before we find ourselves craving a drink or a drug.

For many addicts, the thought of being alone for more than a few minutes is terrifying. In today's high tech world, we are encouraged to be constantly "connected." There is an emphasis on busyness, productivity, and communication that is unique to our era, and this focus constantly affects our choices. To turn our backs on technology and step away from social networking even for a day feels like we are betraying everyone in our circles. "Where were you?" people demand to know, if we dare to log out and unplug. And with the advent of smartphones, there's no longer any excuse for not replying to an email instantaneously. Failing to check our messages is tantamount to leaving the country in the eyes of our employers and associates. Even as we put down the alcohol, drugs, and pills, we become addicted to status updates, alerts, and flashing signals that signify someone somewhere has noticed our existence and has responded to it. We feel obligated to stay current, keeping on top of all "breaking news," lest we be left behind. We must be aware of which celebrities said and did which things, what they wore and with whom they slept; otherwise, we risk becoming "out of touch" and irrelevant. Where keeping up with the Joneses used to refer to owning a home or a certain appliance, it now refers to the mandatory, 24/7 assimilation of information, trends, and public opinion. Going off on our own to "think about stuff" sounds like a dangerous, foolhardy mission at best, and a sign of depression at worst.

LEARNING TO LOVE ONE'S SELF

Even though we are human animals, many of us feel alienated from the natural world. We may feel more at home surrounded by gadgets than we do when in contact with trees, dirt, bugs, sky, and wind. Even on a hike to the top of a mountain, the sight of the bars on our phone tapering off as our connection to "the world" weakens gives us the chills. "Does this forest have Wi-Fi?" we hear ourselves asking, a little too anxiously. With all the texting, IMing, Facebooking, emailing, and photo-sharing life seemingly requires, we have little time to contemplate the deeper issues of our lives, really getting to know ourselves in an intimate way. Solitude is for monks, we say. What place does it have in a modern society? Here, it's good to recall our little green shoot of solitude. Despite centuries of agricultural, industrial, and technological revolution, living things still function in much the same ways that they have since the beginning of time.

For most of my years as an addict, I was obsessed with receiving approval and validation from outside sources. I looked to other people, to products and procedures, and (of course) to alcohol to make me feel good about myself. But this approach to boosting self-worth only caused me to meet with grave disappointment. To know our real value, we have to look inside, cliché as that may sound. Even when we are showered with love, fame, fortune, awards, invitations, gifts, and compliments, it's never enough to convince us that we deserve the good in our lives. We consume these outward displays of affection and then hungrily return for more, exhausting our friends, families, and colleagues with our constant pleas for recognition.

Luckily, there is a deep well of fuel for our egos right within our own souls. It turns out that we can give ourselves the attention we sorely need; in truth, this is the only way to really heal the wounds of low self-esteem. It's ironic, rather like Dorothy discovering she was wearing the ruby slippers all along. Solitude then, is the key to building up our supply of self-love. You can think of time spent alone like a deposit into the bank of self-confidence. Every time you take five minutes to meditate, journal, go on a solo nature walk, or relax in a hot bath, you are amassing wealth—the wealth of the spirit. You are making an investment in your recovery and in your future.

CULTIVATING SOLITUDE

Of course, engaging in solitude will not always cater to an addict's desire for instant gratification. It takes time to reap the benefits of our attempts at meditation and introspection. We need to view the process as worthwhile. It's no secret that food grown slowly, without pesticides, chemicals, or genetic modifications tastes the best. Once we're truly sick of mental, emotional, and spiritual malnutrition, we will be ready and willing to start our journey into solitude, knowing that the fruits of our efforts will be reaped in our lives as joy, peace, and gratitude—states of being that were quite hard to come by during our days of drinking and using.

Solitude is closely related to the other core principles discussed in this book. To be authentic, we must first know what we think and feel before being able to share these insights with others. Solitude helps us to know our own hearts and minds. It's the same with being honest: we need privacy to inwardly review the fears, insecurities, and unfulfilled desires that cause us to lie to ourselves and to others. We need to align with our inner compass and intuition, and when our lives are noisy with television, multimedia, gossip, and drama, we can't hear the voice of our conscience. Without this inner connection, it's as though we are living with a stranger inside.

The relationship between evolution and solitude is also essential. In order to know our dreams and ambitions, we need to spend time exploring our hobbies, wandering around wondering about the world, allowing ourselves the freedom to try new things without having to please anyone or conform to anyone else's schedule or demands. So much of what we want to accomplish requires hours spent studying, practicing, making notes, or performing experiments, all of which require solitude. When we talk about time management in the next chapter, we will begin by addressing the specifics of how to carve out time and space for solitude. Ultimately, when we allot a generous portion of time to nourishing our spirit, we are energized to complete all our other tasks, getting twice as much work done in half the time.

SOLITUDE AND RELATIONSHIPS

In terms of healthy relationships, there is nothing more necessary to sustaining long-term partnerships—romantic, platonic, professional, or otherwise—than the principle of solitude. When two people come together as separate wholes, they can feed each other from the rich sanctuary of ideas, energy, and emotions cultivated in solitude. These are the relationships that can flourish—both parties are independent, able to give and receive without fear of being drained or depleted. In other words, they have boundaries. They know where they end and where the other begins. They are self-defined, rather than defined by their relationship or by their partner's idea of who they should be.

By contrast, in a relationship of dependence, neither party is willing to spend time alone. The resulting "partnership" more closely resembles a hostage situation rather than one of mutual respect. Each person is desperate to get the love they need from the other, resorting to control and manipulation to squeeze more juice out of their "source." These dynamics choke the life out of the relationship, and often precipitate a violent end, as one party or the other hits "rock bottom." It's natural to want to spend every moment with someone you adore, but the reality is that we each come into this world alone and leave it alone; we may get married, have children, start business partnerships or artistic collaborations, but we can never completely merge with other people. We must retain a portion of our identity and energy for ourselves alone, a sacred fortress into which we can retreat at any time in order to become centered.

If you happen to be single, the best thing you can do is to begin dating yourself. For a lot of us, this statement makes us want to cringe. "Are you kidding? Eat out at a fancy restaurant all by myself? What will people say?" The truth is that dating yourself will give you more information about your ideal partner than any number of surveys you could fill out online. Going out and doing things in the world is a way to find out what makes you laugh, what makes you excited, and what makes you bored. How can you communicate these facts to a partner if you're not aware of what activities you like and don't like?

Secondly, getting out in the world is the best way to meet other active, healthy people. Please believe me when I say that you do *not* want to pair up with someone who surfs dating websites night and day for available singles. It may be old-fashioned, but bonds formed in real space and real-time remain the strongest, and the most likely to succeed. So, if you're out treating yourself to a delicious meal on a Saturday night and you start to wonder what people might think, consider this: They are probably saying to themselves, "What I wouldn't give for a night out away from my spouse and kids!" Remember that you won't be single forever, and you will truly miss these golden days of freedom once you're in a committed relationship with all its attendant obligations. The grass is really greenest right where you're standing!

As a counselor conducting therapy sessions all day, solitude is of special importance in my career. I regularly take 15-minute walks throughout the day between my sessions just to clear my head, get calm, and feel like I truly have something to offer my next client. If I fail to engage in healthy solitude, I can become scattered, irritable, and restless. As with the other principles, our brains can be rewired to enjoy small, potent injections of alone time. Experiment by taking five minutes during your lunch break to sit on the grass and draw a picture. Don't show it to anyone; it's for your eyes only. Sure, you might have missed the daily gossip at the water cooler, but just like our metaphorical plant, your leaves will perk up and you just might start showing a few pink buds as the week progresses. Now, instead of dreading being alone, I look forward to it eagerly all week. I spend time running, hiking, going to museums, and reading books. I turn off my phone and my computer, leave my iPod at home, and spend time listening to the sounds of nature, admiring her majestic colors, patterns, and textures. I feel grounded in my senses, and this serenity feeds my sobriety much like alcohol fed my addiction.

Real Recovery: Shayla

I will tell you the story of one of my clients named Shayla. She was a constant consumer of food, alcohol, and television, but she was also addicted to companionship. As a lovely and likeable woman, Shayla was always surrounded by people. When they left, however, she would panic. She hated being alone with her thoughts because they led her to an unwelcome truth: her drinking was out of control and there were consequences to her behavior, namely two DUIs and countless fights with her family.

Shayla's recovery plan needed to emphasize the importance of building a relationship with herself through solitude. After many sessions, she was finally willing to admit that her life was out of control. She also disclosed that she had never had the experience of enjoying a good book or taking a walk by herself—simple pleasures that are so easily taken for granted. I suggested that she devote 10 minutes to one hour every day to being by herself so that she could begin shoring up some serenity and start getting to know herself better. Spending time by herself in a relaxed, healthy way allowed her to slow down, breathe, hear her thoughts, and realize how much she wanted to change her life and move forward. Shayla began with 10 minutes a day and now gives herself regular time every week to enjoy a bath, hike, read, and meditate. The time alone has almost entirely negated her need to overindulge in food, alcohol, TV, and constant companionship. She describes the experience as something akin to awakening from a coma. It is remarkable to watch someone go through this process and emerge with such wonderful, healthy results.

SOLITUDE VS. ISOLATION

Some readers may question whether I am encouraging people to isolate. The distinction between solitude and isolation is an important one. Isolation is common amongst addicts, and it's easy to mistake one for the other, since they both involve spending time alone. But isolation, rather than being a purposeful act of self-love, self-discovery, and adventure, is a fear-based act of hiding out. Too afraid to face life or other people, the isolator will evade invitations, avoid social contact, and make decisions in a vacuum. Isolation is not an empowered choice a person makes in order to facilitate personal growth, and there is nothing therapeutic about it. It is often the result of holding onto dark secrets from our past that cause us to believe we are outcasts.

In solitude, by contrast, we are affirming our worth and value, taking stock of our purpose in life, and nurturing the qualities that make us unique. In isolation, we are merely affirming our alienation from other people.

When I was in my addiction, I began isolating. I would come home from a party just so I could drink more. I would make excuses so I could stay home, and I would cancel plans all the time. If I had scheduled a date or dinner, I would wind up backing out at the last minute; I was nervous that I would not be able to drink the way I wanted to. I also feared drinking too much and being judged. So instead, I isolated; I became introverted and relished the sorrow that behavior brought me. I was sad. I knew I was being unhealthy by doing this, but I felt I had no other way of dealing with life.

The healthy things I used to do were no longer a part of this alone time. If I was alone at home, I was drinking. I was so scared to just sit with my thoughts. I had to be distracting myself in some way. I was uncomfortable physically. The day after a heavy drinking night was always filled with severe anxiety. In San Francisco, I would disappear into a movie theater to watch a film by myself. On the way to the theater, I would walk past a liquor store and decide to take a few little bottles of wine with me. I could not comfortably sit through a 90-minute film unless I had a drink. But I would still be excited to sit in the dark of the theater, usually in the middle of the day since I was not working. I would try to disappear into the story the film. I would drink and sometimes not really remember parts of certain movies I saw during that time period.

One thing I do know was that when the movie was about to end, I would panic. The lights would come on and I would have to face where my life was heading. I would have to deal with my family who was concerned about me and knew something was not right. I would also have to face the endless, spiritless cycle I had gotten myself accustomed to. I so desperately wanted to stop, yet had no insight into how to do so.

Today, I know the difference between isolation and healthy solitude. There is no anxiety or coping, no soothing with alcohol. If I have a long flight or feel tired, I use solitude in order to relieve my stress. I take an hour to unwind, go grocery shopping, and do things to take care of myself, so that I can once more connect with friends and family from a place of renewal. My own mental, physical, emotional, and spiritual health is my top priority. It may take slightly longer to feel better than it did when I used alcohol to cope, but the improvements to my life are well worth it. Every time I practice healing solitude, I am building pathways in my brain that make it easier and easier to live sober long term.

Are you ready for a challenge? I invite you to choose one 24-hour period this week, during which you will completely disconnect from your computer, phone, tablet, social media accounts, and email. You will not have any access to television, video games, or media of any kind. You won't go shopping or engage in any addictions. You will simply spend the whole day alone, doing something incredibly wonderful for yourself that you "never have time for," whatever that may be. Go spend a day at a Buddhist temple in meditation, and enjoy a vegetarian feast in an outdoor garden. Travel to the beach and spend the day listening to the waves, collecting seashells, and breathing in the salty air. Take a new book to the top of the tallest hill you can find and read it under the shade of a tree. Lock yourself in an art studio and finish a painting. Whatever moves you, whatever feels like a revelation, do it. If anyone makes a fuss about your unscheduled absence, ignore them! This is *your* day! Turn your back on all the drama of this world and, for just one cycle of the sun, abandon all other priorities save that of meeting yourself in the deepest palace chambers of your heart.

The next day, write down your experiences. Did you feel anxious? Stupid? Undeserving? Did you experience odd physical aches and pains when you put yourself first? Were you excited? What did you find out about yourself? Continue your exploration by completing the questions on the next page. Always remember that you are building new pathways in your brain; like building new muscles, you have to practice these new behaviors often until they become habits. There will be discomfort, and there will be moments of frustration, but you will emerge as a stronger, more confident, and introspective person who enjoys spending time alone just as much as spending time with others. You will be restored to a state of balance and peace.

Questions for Exploration: SOLITUDE

- How much time do you spend by yourself?

- Do you fear being alone?

- Do you find it painful and difficult to tell others when you need to separate?

- Are you connected to technology 24/7? Do you go into withdrawal if your Internet connection fails?

- How can you comfort and nurture yourself on a daily basis?

- What new things have you discovered about yourself since implementing the principle of solitude?

- In what areas of your life do you need to cultivate more serenity and peace? In what areas have you been successful at doing this?

- Are you attracted to drama?

- What would it feel like if there were no drama in your life?

- Do you lean toward isolation?

- What changes have you experienced upon spending more time with yourself?

- Write a letter to yourself as a child; then write a letter to yourself at 90. What messages do these selves have for you in the present?

Chapter 5

TIME MANAGEMENT

"Until you value yourself, you won't value your time. Until you value your time, you will not do anything with it."

—M. Scott Peck

For most of us, time is an enemy—a constant obstacle to our serenity. We live at odds with time, always either running out of it or trying (and failing) to manipulate it; we may even choose to ignore it completely. If we're young, we want time to speed up, so that we can finally be independent. If we're older, we try to defy time by refusing to age gracefully. No matter where we are driving, we insist on getting there as quickly as possible, yelling and honking just to shave a few seconds off our route. We suffer through the monotony of the workweek, then party into the wee hours of the weekend, returning exhausted on Monday to repeat the cycle. Our bosses, friends, and families all place demands on our schedule, and it can start to feel like we are losing control of our lives. Rarely do we exist in the present moment. Living in harmony with time is just not in our repertoire.

Likewise, the concept of "doing nothing" repulses us. Stillness makes us shudder. There is a deep undercurrent in our culture that equates self-worth with productivity and achievement. If we are not constantly busy with improving ourselves—our appearances, our incomes, our resumes—we feel an unspoken indictment that we are lazy, unmotivated, and mediocre. By comparison, in some countries such as Spain, Italy, and the Philippines, workers take a *siesta* in the middle of the workday. Shops and businesses lock their doors while employees go home to enjoy a nap, a delicious home-cooked meal, and some time with friends and family. They then return to their jobs refreshed and satiated, and not once have their economies suffered as a result. This lifestyle is almost unimaginable to most of us. The demands of the workplace are pitted against our basic needs for sleep, relaxation, and downtime, and it's not uncommon for the ambitious company man or woman to put in upward of 60 hours a week at the office. In extreme cases, self-care is viewed as weakness, or a lack of commitment.

So it's no wonder that, as addicts, we struggle to organize our lives in a balanced, compassionate way that includes time for sleep, fun, hanging out, reading, *and* doing nothing. When we decide to tackle the issue of managing our time, we are striking out into the unknown, swimming against the current. It's daunting to admit this part of our life needs an overhaul, but unless we face this important element, we will continue to drink and use, just to meet the unreasonable demands of an existence someone else has created for us.

Real Recovery: Kathy

Kathy, a former client of mine, struggled particularly with creating healthy boundaries around time. She was a born people-pleaser. Putting the needs of others before her own was easy and automatic for her. Kathy seemed to have no concept of the word "No." She constantly felt drained and never seemed to have time to herself. Her only reward came at the end of the day when she engaged in binge eating. Unhappy with her weight gain and loss of energy, she came to see me.

It soon became obvious that overeating was just a symptom of Kathy's dysfunctional relationship with time. Her recovery plan included an emphasis on better management of the hours in her day, so that she could prioritize and focus on her own needs. She learned how to set limits on the time she spent helping her children, her husband, and the many charities with which she was involved. We broke down how she was currently spending her time and how she could restructure her days and weeks so that she received the same love and respect she generously doled out to others. By devoting more time to what she wanted to do for herself, she came to rely less on Ben & Jerry's for comfort, and as her weight improved, she began to feel a sense of joy for the first time in years

In my own experience with time management, the last couple months of my addiction were a blur. I did not manage my time at all. I would try to hurry through a day so that the night would arrive and I could drink. When I couldn't get the hours to pass quickly enough, I would take matters into my own hands and drink in the late afternoons. Then when late afternoon was taking too long, I would drink at noon. My time was not valued. I would procrastinate and avoid doing anything that wasn't urgent. I hid from all types of self care, from seeing a dentist or doctor to avoiding anyone or anything where I might be confronted about my drinking. The pain of all this hiding and lying was excruciating. I hated the lies. Days would eventually bleed into one another. There were even times when I did not know which day it was at all. My drinking had gotten that bad.

When I got sober, valuing my time and energy, and taking care of tasks became a top priority. I had myself on a strict schedule of sorts. I began running in the mornings. It helped me physically reconnect with my body, made my mind strong, and it gave me a chance to reflect on my intentions for the day, and what was going on in my life. I went to bed at a specific time, around 10–10:30 pm, to make sure I got enough rest and sleep. I had to explain to family, friends, and the people I worked for that my well-being was non-negotiable. I could not compromise my health, and we should never be expected to do so.

RECAPTURING TIME

Perhaps the best way to begin healing our relationship with time is to begin thinking about our natural rhythms. From the four seasons to the moon's phases to our own heartbeats, there is an underlying pulse to life on Earth that is both comforting and beautiful. When we are children, we learn to think of the day and the night as dance partners, trading places each 24-hour period. The revolutions of the planets and the motion of the waves encircle us like a cosmic embrace. Most of us encounter music for the first time as kids, and the beat of the drum, tambourine, or bass delights us. Deep inside we feel connected to time.

In order to recapture the magic of living in tune with the rhythms of the universe, we have to stop defying time and start *respecting* it. A perfect gauge of this relationship is our breathing. If we are not breathing enough, or breathing shallowly, we can oftentimes find ourselves off the beat. As an exercise, try sitting down and just breathing naturally. You will find that your chest rises and falls to your own rhythm, without force. It is the song of *you*. When you hold your breath, whether out of dread, anxiety, or in order not to feel, you interrupt this music of life and cause yourself stress. Breathing in and out, normally and easily, will instantly ground you in your body, in your life, and in time.

The second thing to remember is that life is essentially a creative process. We create our own realities. We are not slaves to time; instead we have the ability to mold and shape our day according to the values we hold most dear. If we say that our priority is our children, but then we can never find the time to play with them, there is a discrepancy between our actions and the intentions in our heart. This imbalance causes pain, and the pain drives us back toward addiction. If our life's goal is to write novels, yet we cannot find even 10 minutes a day to devote to our dream, we have a problem with time management.

Luckily, there are some excellent tools we can use to help redistribute our time and make sure the things we truly care about are receiving adequate representation in our day. These include time tracking, creating a time spending plan or pie chart, and the use of micro actions.

TIME TRACKING

If you've ever seriously tried to lose weight, then you've probably stepped onto a scale at some point. You felt that you needed to know with certainty what the number was. Perhaps you were surprised and discovered you really weren't as heavy as you thought. Conversely, you may have been horrified to discover your weight was much higher than you expected. Either way, the clarity gained by using a scale is invaluable. It takes the problem out of the realm of conjecture and roots it firmly in mathematics. There's no more hiding, minimizing, exaggerating, or lying. Facts are facts.

It's the same with our time. We need to take an x-ray of our broken schedule in order to figure out where the injury originates. The only way to do this is to literally write down each activity, from morning to night, along with how long it takes us. There are some great phone apps that will help you do this; otherwise you have only to carry around a little notebook. By the end of three days, you will have enough information to connect the dots. You can take an average of each activity and know exactly how many hours you spend traveling, eating, shopping, watching TV, playing games, chatting on the phone, and doing chores. The object isn't to judge or censor yourself, but rather to act as a scientist, measuring and recording where all the hours and minutes go. After you've done this, you will have enough data to begin working on your time spending plan.

Time Spending Plan

Just as you create a budget for your money, you can create a time budget. Each of us is given a fixed time income: 24 hours a day, or 168 hours a week. Having completed our time recording exercise, we will have a rough idea of our time "expenses." Let's say that we will typically need about 52 hours of sleep each week. If we have a set work schedule of 30 hours a week, we are left with 86 remaining hours. We can subtract the activities that are mandatory, such as grocery shopping and pet care. Finally, we will get down to some flexible, "free" hours. How will we spend them?

Here, we can make a list of all the pleasurable, self-nourishing activities we would like to fit into our week: exercise, writing, playing music, socializing, dating, cooking, meditating, etc. We immediately notice that there *is* enough time—maybe not enough to do *everything*, but certainly enough to do a few things each week that reflect our authentic, innermost self.

Micro-actions

The biggest obstacle that holds most people back from creating the life of their dreams is the idea that they can only write, paint, dance, read, go to school, or play music if they have a significant block of time to devote to the activity. Unfortunately, those large blocks of time may never manifest. What we're left with is our fantasies and no results.

That's where micro-actions come into play. If I told you that you could finish a novel by writing for 10 minutes a day for three months, how would that make you feel? Empowered? Terrified? Skeptical? The truth is that consistently sitting down at the computer for 10 minutes every single day is a goal that even the busiest person can achieve. And, regardless of how you feel about doing so, if you commit to it, you *will* produce a novel. It's just simple math.

Let's take another example: exercise. You have a 40-hour-a-week job, two kids, and you're in school on the weekend. How can you make it happen? Micro-actions to the rescue! Use 10 minutes from your lunch hour. Bring a floor mat and find a place to do abs. Every time you see a staircase, use it. Find opportunities to walk someplace instead of driving. It will all add up. You may not be able to look like a toned and sculpted celebrity, but your body will thank you. And I promise, you will feel better about yourself than if you had spent those 10 minutes a day on Facebook!

Granted, micro-actions can wreak havoc on our egos, which prefer grand, sweeping gestures—whole weekends locked in an art studio, *creating*—to 20 minutes of drawing while stuck in traffic on the freeway. Nevertheless, micro-actions *will* produce results, and they *will* transform your life. They will open up all kinds of possibilities you never knew were possible. There are several famous photographers who got their start just photographing the people they saw on their way to work.

The same goes for relationships. You may not have time to go see a movie and have dinner, but you can always think of small, romantic ways to keep the spark alive, such as handwriting a love letter to your spouse and dropping it in the mail. Instead of cursing our lack of time, we can practice the principle of humility and accept small, consistent baby steps forward over dramatic leaps.

PROCRASTINATION

Sometimes, time management problems can function as a mask or diversion, distracting us from facing a deeper issue. I once had a client who was chronically late to her appointments. She blamed it on traffic or her work schedule, but I began to suspect there was something else going on. Eventually it came out that she was angry about a comment I had made in passing months earlier. Being too polite to risk conflict, the woman had simply buried her rage and was instead manifesting her frustration through tardiness. Once we were able to resolve her negative feelings, she suddenly started showing up promptly each week.

Procrastination is another sign that we may be avoiding uncomfortable feelings. Perhaps the thought of completing a certain task fills us with fear. Rather than risk failure (or success), we simple put off the encounter for another day. Sometimes the fantasy of the future is more comforting to us than the reality. Being a musician may seem like a noble ambition until we actually have to put in the daily hours of practice. The task quickly becomes mundane, so we delay. These are all very natural human responses to moving forward in life, but with support we can overcome procrastination and settle into a deeper intimacy with our goals.

One of the best methods I've found for dealing with procrastination is the Action Subdivision Method. This is the tactic of breaking down any overwhelming action into small, manageable components that you can easily accomplish. For instance, let's say you need to complete an errand that you absolutely dread. Step one is getting into the car. Once you've done that, congratulate yourself. Step one is complete. Next comes starting the vehicle. Done! Now you might divide your drive into thirds, followed by parking, walking to the door, and entering. Altogether, your dreaded errand may consist of little more than the eight mini-actions that you took, each completely manageable on its own. This may sound absurd, but it's highly effective. It may even make you giggle!

Taking responsibility for the way you use time may cause some feelings of frustration and resentment at first. After all, you will no longer be able to play the victim, complain about your impossible work schedule or come up with excuses. You will have to call forth a new level of honesty as you set boundaries with others, let go of activities that don't serve your life's purpose and defect from the league of shadow dreamers who are more comfortable watching television, drinking, or overeating than daring to inch toward their heart's authentic vision. This new relationship to time will feel completely counterintuitive at first, but just remember that our brains are outstandingly adaptable to forming new habits.

As with all the elements in this book, rewiring is the secret to lasting and dynamic change. When you learn a new way of relating to time, you are altering your neural connections. Every time you practice self-care, balance, and mindfulness of the present moment, your synapses are gobbling up the new input and growing strong, healthy grooves to reinforce the new behavior. On the following page, you will find some additional questions to help you explore the concept of time management in greater depth. This week's assignment is to practice just one of the tools outlined in this chapter for just one day. Good luck!

Questions for Exploration: **TIME MANAGEMENT**

- How do you allocate your time each day? How many hours a day does your work require? How do you spend the time outside of work?

- Does your work drain you of your energy or does it give you a purpose, enjoyment, and hope?

- To whom do you give your energy on a daily basis? Do these individuals add light to your life or do they deplete you of your energy?

- How might you restructure your time and energy so that you have more of both to spend on taking care of yourself—in mind, body, and spirit?

- In what areas of your life do you procrastinate?

- Do you suffer from chronic tardiness? What do you think is the root cause?

- Is your life in balance? Do you feel that any one area is lacking in attention?

- What dream or aspirations are you willing to work toward in small steps?

- What does it feel like when you are truly present in the moment?

Chapter 6

SELF-CARE

"But this revolutionary act of treating ourselves tenderly can begin to undo the aversive messages of a lifetime."

—TARA BRACH

"Nourishing yourself in a way that helps you blossom in the direction you want to go is attainable, and you are worth the effort."

—DEBORAH DAY

Kim felt lazy, out of shape, mentally stagnant, and emotionally empty. She no longer worked out, she had stopped reading, going out on dates, seeing friends, and playing the piano, all of which she had once adored. She had lost her momentum in life and had stopped caring for herself. Her only coping mechanism had become the regular use of sleeping pills and alcohol. She had fallen into a deep, dark abyss. This was the state I found Kim in when she came to see me. I immediately recognized that her recovery needed to focus on self-care, so I designed a treatment plan that would address self-love in all areas—mental, phys-ical, emotional, and spiritual.

Kim agreed to let go of the dead-end substances, at least temporarily, while she explored some of my suggestions for new kinds of activities. She began by taking yoga and stretching daily to reconnect with her body. This provided such positive results that Kim felt open to learning other ways she could be mindful of her physical well being. She added soothing baths and also started seeing a physical therapist for her back pains. As she slowly started to feel better, Kim found herself reaching out to old friends, reading books that inspired her, and generally feeling more productive. By focusing her recovery plan on self-care, she was able to feel healthier and more vital on all levels. Soon the pills and booze were a thing of the past.

If you can identify with Kim's story, you are not alone. Speaking personally, self-care was not something I excelled at in the midst of my addiction. I did not value my time, body, mind, or spirit. I would wander around, fantasizing about working out. I even attempted to join a gym. I would force myself to walk there after work. Sadly, whenever I completed one of the painstaking exercise routines, I would celebrate the only way I knew how—with a drink. It was completely counterproductive.

Self-care may especially elude us if our basic needs were neglected or denied as children. We simply recreate the deprivation and stagnation of our youth, unaware of the alternatives. When our needs went unfulfilled, we may have developed a sense of undeserving, believing that somewhere inside we lack worth. We mistakenly believed *we* were the cause of the cruelty or coldness at home, and this low self-esteem and self-loathing now informs all our daily activities. If we grew up listening to our parents fight as we fell asleep, or we had to sleep with one eye open because we were terrified of our caregivers, we may find something as basic as a good night's rest eludes us as an adult. Similarly, if we grew up as a latchkey kid, we may not know how to nourish ourselves with friendships or relationships, preferring instead to isolate because that's what feels most familiar. As far as self-care goes, many of us are starting from scratch.

YOUR HIERARCHY OF NEEDS

A psychologist named Abraham Maslow created a "hierarchy of needs" shaped like a pyramid, which described the basic needs of all humans, ranked by their relative importance. He placed physiological needs like sleep, food, sex, excretion, and clean air and water on the lowest level, as he considered them the most necessary for survival. The next level dealt with security and safety, and included such things as employment, health, and property. The third level was composed of needs for belonging, such as friendship, intimacy, and family, with the fourth and fifth pyramid rungs reserved for needs corresponding to self-esteem and self-actualization. On these last levels he included the need for respect, achievement, and creativity.

You may not be a psychologist, but you too can create your own pyramid just by writing down a list of what you believe is required in your life to make you happy and healthy. The process of writing these items down can turn the daunting task of self-care into something manageable, finite, and pleasant, rather than vague and infinite. For my list, I might mention sleep, food, friendship, knowledge, recreation, down time, alone time, time with family, self-improvement, and travel. Yours may be different. In this way you can create a personalized self-care checklist, arranging your needs according to urgency. When you do something kind for yourself, you can make a checkmark on your list. If you start small but stick with it, over time you will begin to notice remarkable changes in your life. Your pyramid will overflow with possibility, joy, and spontaneity, as you come to know real satisfaction in living. This is something addiction could never provide, no matter how loyal you remained to the substance or behavior that was supposed to make things better.

As your brain makes the mental switch from "How can I punish or harm myself?" to "How can I love myself?" you will start investing in your new lifestyle with all the enthusiasm and passion that you once reserved for using. Instead of boasting about how much you drank over the weekend, you may find yourself showing off the amazing new pillows you bought that make you sleep like an angel! It's all a matter of perspective, but one thing is certain: Learning to value yourself as precious, lovable, and worthy of exquisite kindness is a solid step toward long-term sobriety.

CARING FOR YOUR PHYSICAL NEEDS

When we think about nourishing the physical body, the first thing that comes to mind is eating well. Many drug users and alcoholics neglect this basic act of self-love, subsisting on junk food, take-out, and in some cases forget to feed themselves altogether. Learning to enjoy three healthy, delicious meals a day can be a wonderful adventure in self-discovery, and cooking itself can be a creative new hobby.

For those addicted to food, self-care may look different. In this case, the compulsive eater must also embark on a process of exploration, but one that seeks out non-edible forms of nourishment that provide equal comfort. Luckily, the realm of the senses is vast. Take our sense of smell: We can feed our "nose buds" with incense, scented candles, fresh flowers, perfumes, garden herbs, or aromatherapy, going on a scavenger hunt to unearth all the smells we find the most pleasing and replenishing.

Too many of us have long neglected our sense of touch. We may never have experienced the joyful release of a therapeutic massage or the delight of a simple bubble bath. Walking barefoot in the hot sand or lying down in a wet field of grass can ground us and connect us to nature in ways we can hardly fathom. Our sense of hearing also needs to be nourished. When was the last time you listened to an opera? The rain beating on the window? Your favorite rock band? We often take our sense of sight for granted, but when you think of your eyes as organs worthy of a feast, you might be inspired to visit an art gallery, climb to the top of a mountain to view a sunset, or stroll through a whimsical antique shop. Addiction narrows our sensual palettes, casting us into a gray netherworld devoid of beauty, delight, and surprise.

As you begin to practice caring for your body and its boundless desire for new stimuli, you may feel as if you're being born for the first time. And, in a way, you are. Every time you practice living in the present moment through nourishing your sense of taste, smell, sight, sound, or touch, you form a new pathway in your brain that is recorded and strengthened. This pathway becomes a blueprint for the future, assuring that so long as you continue your new self-nourishing behaviors, you will no longer feel the need to numb out with substances. The present will have become a safe and rewarding place, rather than a nightmare from which to flee.

SEEING TO YOUR MENTAL NEEDS

The mind, like the body, can also suffer from malnutrition. During addiction, we often stop growing intellectually, too preoccupied with getting our next fix, controlling and manipulating other people, or numbing out with the "mental junk food" of too much TV or too many video games. In recovery, we can start to feed our brains the rich, fulfilling cuisine of great books and new skills, striving each day to stretch and broaden our minds. After all, the mind is a muscle, and without exercise it will suffer and atrophy. Reading is difficult for some because it requires concentration, imagination and sitting still. But there remains a reason why people still write and read books despite all the other forms of entertainment and media. Some stories just need to be told in the unique format of a written manuscript. Reading a book can be a very intense, private, and introspective experience, something to savor over weeks rather than hours. The much-adored author J.D. Salinger once remarked, "What really knocks me out is a book that, when you're all done reading it, you wish the author that wrote it was a terrific friend of yours and you could call him up on the phone whenever you felt like it." This feeling of connection is an excellent reason to invest time in reading.

You may be skeptical as to whether aging adult brains can learn new tricks. According to the latest scientific research, the real culprits in poor learning outcomes are due to perfectionism, low self-esteem, and a lack of time invested. At the University of Nevada, a study revealed that when adults were told they had above average athletic skills, their confidence actually improved their performance, even if they had never played a sport before. In short, there is absolutely no reason why you can't learn a language or an instrument, return to school, or master a sport, even if you've never done anything similar in your whole life. With the right amount of encouragement, you are just as much a "sponge" for new knowledge as a 7-year-old child. This growth and expansion of the mind falls into the category of Evolution, which we discussed in Chapter 3. You may be starting to understand that each of the principles in this book represents a different form of self-care. Recovery *is* self-care!

Exercise as Self-Care

Exercise is a form of self-care that is both physical and mental. Have you ever been around an animal that has been cooped up too long? It becomes angry and territorial, or even depressed and listless. Human beings are no different. You may have neglected your need for exercise for so long that you don't even notice the effect the shortage is having on your personality.

The good news is that you don't have to rush out and become the next Olympic athlete overnight. Any form of vigorous movement will do, even just going for a brisk walk. Find something fun that doesn't feel like a chore and get into it. Most YMCAs have regular volleyball teams, handball courts, and pools. Even playing the drums can be a form of exercise. If you like to dance, get to the club every week and work out your need for exercise there. Movement itself is healing. It gets you thinking on your feet, which translates into every area of life, increasing your confidence and preventing your vital energy from pooling up in the mind. Just try to exercise like a kid, without regard for anything but the sheer pleasure of mobilizing your limbs and expressing your aliveness.

EMOTIONAL AND SPIRITUAL SELF-CARE

Like Maslow, we must also acknowledge our need for more subtle and sophisticated forms of self-care, beyond just the physical and mental. Human beings, as intelligent life forms, harbor a deep need for existential meaning, for making sense of our place in the universe. How do we go about nourishing ourselves emotionally and spiritually? How do we attend to our hearts and souls?

There are as many routes to this type of self-actualization as there are types of people. Some will find that guided meditation on a certain topic is their key to a sense of balance and serenity, while others find solace in religious activities or rituals. Sometimes just getting out of our comfort zone and exploring a Catholic cathedral, a Native American sweat lodge, a Wiccan drum circle, or even attending a lecture on astronomy can lead to all kinds of brilliant insights and breakthroughs. Volunteering, be it at an animal shelter or a home for the elderly, is another option; not only is volunteering a gift for you, but for others, too. Whatever direction you decide upon, remember that curiosity and a sense of wonder will dissolve long-held barriers that may be keeping you bored, sad, or feeling empty.

Believe it or not, even crying can be a form of self-care. Allowing yourself to fully process grief can be a cathartic and rewarding process, despite our cultural preference for sanitized emotions. In Spanish,

Italian, and Arab cultures, mourning is nothing to be ashamed of; in fact, weeping at funerals is even a profession! People from those countries tend to fight loud and make up just as passionately. They do not stifle feelings, and there are a lot of benefits to be gained from letting yourself feel your emotions.

If you've never tried primal screaming, you may be in for a treat. You can do this alone in your car, into your pillow, or at a secluded beach. Just scream at the top of your lungs, releasing all the pent up frustration and rage of a lifetime. It feels great! Or maybe, instead of crying or screaming, you need to care for yourself with laughter. When was the last time you laughed so hard you thought you might pee in your pants? Get yourself to a comedy club or a funny movie. Crack open a joke book, just like you did when you were 8. Play a practical joke on a friend or co-worker when they least expect it. Make funny faces at a baby. Laughter truly is medicine for the soul.

SELF-CARE WITHOUT SELF-CENTEREDNESS

As a final note, remember that there is a big difference between self-care and selfishness. There may be plenty of people who resent your sudden shift in priorities. They will try to call you names, such as "self-centered" or "narcissistic," just because you want to spend the day taking care of yourself and your needs, instead of others. It can be very discouraging when these comments come from people close to us. Here, the analogy of the oxygen mask on an airplane serves us well. How can you give to others if you yourself are completely drained of all joy, energy, and peace? In the first stages of recovering from any addiction, we are depleted—physically, emotionally, mentally, and spiritually. Our only job is to heal. This doesn't mean you should shirk your responsibilities entirely, but don't underestimate the size of the deficit in self-love that has formed over the years. It will take a genuine investment of your time and attention to begin filling up your reserves with positive, healthy new habits. Unless you devote yourself to self-care as though your life depends upon it, it's easy to fall prey to relapse; the old habits die hard.

Gently setting boundaries with friends and family members is a must. In time, they will come to appreciate your commitment to recovery and reap the benefits of your renewed sense of self, your comfort in your own skin, and the pleasure you take in their company, now that you are truly present. In the next chapter, you will learn more about practicing self-care around personal relationships. You can also refer to Chapter 11: Affirmations and Intentions to assist you on your journey to self-love. Lastly, the questions you find on the following page will also aid in the exploration process.

Questions for Exploration: SELF-CARE

- What is the most important thing you can do today to exercise self-care?

- In what ways have you neglected yourself during your active addiction?

- What steps can you take to nourish and nurture you physical body? Your mind? Your heart and emotions? Your spirit?

- What were the results? How did you feel before, during, and after?

- How can you do for yourself the things you wish others would do for you?

- How often do you say yes when you mean no? How often do you do the opposite?

- Who are your allies that will support your new regimen of self-care?

- How can you better care for yourself at work?

- What are your personal danger signals that you are slipping back into your old ways?

- How can you reward yourself for your progress on a daily basis?

Chapter 7

HEALTHY RELATIONSHIPS

"The purpose of a relationship is not to have another who might complete you, but to have another with whom you might share your completeness."

—NEALE DONALD WALSCH

Life is all about relationships. They are a crucial part of human experience. When we are young, we take our cues from the people surrounding us. We rely on them to make us feel validated, seen, heard, and loved. We need community, a village, or a support system of some kind, to develop and grow into healthy adults. If we didn't get this initially, we will need to recreate it in adulthood, if we are to achieve sobriety. Luckily, once we have established a strong, stable relationship with ourselves through the principles of Authenticity, Honesty, Evolution, Solitude, Time Management, and Self-Care, we are well on our way to manifesting such a community. A wonderful new world full of profound and harmonious connections awaits us on the other side. The new friendships and partnerships we form now will be based on the bedrock of recovery rather than on dependency and fear, and they are rewarding beyond our wildest dreams.

To reach this point, however, we must begin to teach others how to treat us. I learned this principle the hard way. Toward the end of my drinking, I had gotten into a relationship that was filled with toxicity. I had met a fellow daily drinker who was a little younger than me and came from a different background. He had grown up around abuse and had adapted by becoming very controlling, as well as developing an addiction to drinking beer and smoking pot. Our relationship quickly became tumultuous and verbally abusive. Although I realized I was compromising the respect I knew I deserved, I continued to remain in this unhealthy relationship, thinking, "Who else would want to be with me? I drink so much. Who else would tolerate me and enable me to continue with this addiction?" He drank just as much as I did, and it let me feel like I had normalized my behavior. I could be "myself" around him. This faulty belief system perpetuated an endless unhealthy cycle.

When I got sober, I finally left him. I vowed I would never have a relationship that was inauthentic again. I took an oath that I would only allow positivity, health, and a feeling of well being in my relationships and personal life. No more toxicity, addiction, trauma, or drama. No more abuse. Today in my life I allow authenticity to be my guiding North Star. I don't put on masks, and I don't allow anyone to threaten my commitment to sobriety. If I begin dating someone and I see that the person has anger issues or any other unhealthy behaviors, I heed the red flags and remove myself from harm's way. I do not tolerate even a modicum of abuse, be it verbal, emotional, or physical. Honesty guides my actions in all of my relationships, romantic and otherwise. I continue to grow spiritually, knowing that whether I am alone or in a partnership, I am learning valuable lessons that will open and heal my heart.

HEALTHY ROMANCE

When it comes to romantic relationships, one of the most important concepts I can share with you is the idea of setting an intention. If you can truly visualize and imagine the type of person you wish to be with, sensing the inner qualities you seek in a mate, you are that much closer to encountering a healthy, happy significant other in real life. A dear friend and colleague of mine named Oliver had been yearning for quite some time for a true and sacred love. He wanted to start a family but could not find a woman that he felt was his match. For years he had a clear feeling about what he wanted in a partner, but he had not met her yet. He was told by a shaman to think of the way he wanted this connection with this woman to feel—what she looked like, her demeanor, etc. He was told to connect with his image of her through thought, emotion, and spirit. The shaman then directed him to set this intention formally by writing it down on a piece of paper and putting it under his pillow every night. He did this over and over, night after night. He thoroughly imagined his love-to-be, envisioning how she sounded, felt, looked—even down to the lightness of her energy.

Months later he was at a wedding and a woman walked up the hill toward him. His dad had met her years before, and knew her family. Oliver said that the minute he saw her, he knew she was the one. She was the woman he had been thinking of! It was an instant connection. She had the same energy he was hoping to find. He swears to this day that by putting his deepest desires into the universe, he was able to draw out a partner who embodied everything he wanted. They have since married, and have two beautiful children and a wonderful partnership. He is a powerful example of the idea that we do not have to settle in personal relationships. We can truly find the love of our lives when we set our minds to it.

CULTIVATING HEALTHY EVERYDAY RELATIONSHIPS

Romantic relationships are not the only ones that improve when we practice the other principles in this book in earnest. Our relationships with co-workers, family members, and even strangers all evolve as well.

However, attempting to move into balance with other people can be quite challenging at first. Addiction is largely a disease of poor boundaries. Recovering addicts tend to either gravitate toward enmeshment with others (too much involvement), or they become overwhelmed and withdraw into isolation (too little involvement). Both are extremes that lack the fulfillment and joy of real intimacy, a state that can only be achieved when we understand the importance of boundaries.

In the case of substance abuse, we lose control over the food, alcohol, or drugs entering our bodies. Non-addicts may have a self-protective mechanism that warns them to stop before they get hurt, but the alcoholic or drug user has no brakes. It follows that our lack of physical, emotional, mental, and spiritual self-care has also spread to our relationships. We may have all kinds of morally bankrupt people in our lives; people who take advantage of us, harm us, neglect us, or pull us back into the darkness. In some cases, there is also a list of people whom we ourselves have mistreated. If we truly want long-term sobriety, we have to take stock of all the relationships in our lives, determining which ones are toxic, which require repair, and which ones nourish and nurture us. You can begin to do this right now, regardless of how long you have been clean.

Try this: Draw three concentric circles on a piece of paper. Let these represent three levels of intimacy. The innermost circle is reserved for the people you trust the most in this world. These people are your rocks, your guardian angels. They will support you in a crisis, tell you the truth even when it's uncomfortable, and make you laugh when you're taking life too seriously. They may be few in quantity, but they make up for it in quality. In the second circle, place the people whom you also trust, but perhaps haven't known as long; and in the third circle you can write down the names of folks you like, but want to know better. This is a very enlightening exercise, as you will notice that it's difficult to write down certain names that you thought might be easy to include. Something about putting things in writing forces us to confront reality in a much deeper, more honest way.

The writing process also teaches us about gray areas in relationships. Not every acquaintance will become an intimate friend, but we have room in life for a variety of intimacy levels. Knowing how and when to move closer or further away is an art, a skill that must be developed and practiced to perfection. Try to visualize the other person as a fire. Some fires are best appreciated at a great distance (like the sun) while others make you want to curl up next to them. Some fires give off constant, reliable warmth and light, while others burn out quickly. Everyone can be appreciated given the right perspective.

Healthy relationships are based on the underlying principle of trust. This is a sore spot for many addicts. We may come from trauma, betrayal, or neglect, and often we have never experienced true caring, reciprocity, or loyalty in our lives. But we can learn to build trust in small, progressive steps, establishing healthy, firm foundations in all our liaisons. In some cases, we may need to take a break from our primary relationships with family, friends, and partners to cleanse our "intimacy palette" with a period of solitude. From there, we can go about reintroducing our loved ones back into our lives, this time on new terms—sober terms. It goes without saying that we want to surround ourselves with people who don't drink or use, those who will honor our recovery by not engaging in those behaviors around us.

RECOVERING RELATIONSHIPS ONE STEP AT A TIME

The main thing to remember is that it's okay to get to know people slowly. In movies and TV shows, we watch people race through this process at lightning speeds. After all, they only have about two hours to meet, fall in love, get married, have children, and get divorced! The heavy influence of film and other media may confuse us as to the real investment it takes to build lasting relationships and to feel safe with others.

So, take your time. Go out for coffee with someone, even if you've known the person a long time, and ask yourself, "How does this person treat me? Do they spend the whole time talking about themselves? Do they always let me pick up the tab? Do they ask how my day was? Do they gossip? Do they share their feelings with me, or keep me at a distance? Do they make me happy? Are they safe?"

It's okay to evaluate others; in fact, it's our responsibility to do so. As you begin this process of discernment, it can be invaluable to have a therapist or counselor to talk to about the people in your life. If we've spent years being a doormat, a caretaker, or a people-pleaser of any kind, it won't be easy to change overnight. Coming into harmony with others mirrors the journey our body must make as it heals from the physical repercussions of alcoholism and drug addiction.

In terms of rewiring, our brains are built just like those of other mammals. When we experience trust, the comforting chemical oxytocin is released. It's this chemical that helps animals bond with groups of their peers, protect their offspring, and establish patterns of reliability and routine. Betrayal thwarts oxytocin, triggering depression, fear, and confusion. Once we've experienced a stab in the back, it can be difficult to motivate ourselves onward to form positive relationships again; but unless we try, we will remain in that state of depression. Chemically, we *need* healthy relationships in order to feel good. So giving up on other people entirely is not an option. What works instead is taking small, manageable steps toward intimacy, allowing our brain's pathways to soak up the positive effects, and then repeating the process.

Real Recovery: Tammy

To give you one last example of just how important healthy relationships are to our sobriety, I will tell you about one of my clients, Tammy. She went through a process that I think you will find especially poignant. Tammy's husband was a heavy drinker. He was both verbally and physically abusive to her. He said cruel things about her weight, her clothes, her family, and her personality. When his verbal abuse didn't satisfy his urge to vent, his anger escalated into physical abuse. He began shoving and slapping Tammy. As she became the main target of his outbursts, Tammy's anxiety skyrocketed. She became depressed and hopeless. She had been taking benzodiazepines—mainly Xanax and Klonopin—prescription pills that she would get from her doctor. Tammy's tolerance to the prescription drugs had increased, however, and she was soon taking up to 10 pills a day. Things got progressively worse—until the afternoon she wrapped her car around a telephone pole. By numbing out the pain in her life, she almost killed herself and others. This was the horrifying result of running from her destructive relationship.

Tammy came to me, and we began the process of healing the trauma of her abuse, physically removing her from this abusive man and the negative energy that was swirling around him. Her recovery plan required an emphasis on healthy friendships and relationships. Tammy moved in with her sister, let go of the acquaintances that were associated with her husband and his manipulative family, and set non-negotiable boundaries. She began to reconnect with the friends and family she had pushed away and had become isolated from. She surrounded herself with positive people and love. As she began to heal, her sobriety grew stronger. Today you would never know that domestic violence was ever a part of her story. She is strong, confident, and wise—a true survivor.

LEARNING TO LEAVE WITH LOVE

In my experience, I have found the only way to detach successfully is to do so with love. It can be difficult, especially when dealing with a person who has caused you so much damage, but you can begin by making a list of gratitudes about the person you need to separate from. Think of all the things they've taught you. If you can't think of anything positive about them, simply focus on how much self-awareness you've gained while knowing them. See this person as a teacher who has enlightened you about how you need to change and grow. With humility and gratitude, find a blessing you can internally wish upon this person. Try to bless them every day until the separation begins to lose some of its power. It's remarkable how much easier it is to detach from others in this manner, rather than with fear, hatred, or rage. Think of the other person as being a rock, dislodged from a riverbed. The water flows softly and gently until the rock is released. It's the opposite of a violent process.

There is much grief associated with the loss of relationships, even toxic ones. So don't underestimate this stage of your recovery. Be extra kind to yourself as you let go of unhealthy unions. You are undergoing social and emotional surgery! Create an ICU for yourself at home with blankets, hot baths, warm tea, and plenty of good books. The grief won't last forever, but it may last a while. Be patient and compassionate with yourself, knowing that solitude cannot harm you. It can only help.

We will further explore relationships with others in the next three chapters on Gratitude, Compassion, and Love, but for now, begin your journey in this area by answering the questions on the next page. None of us become experts at relationships overnight. All we can do is to ask questions, record our experiences and try to learn from our mistakes. We are all in the same boat in this world, trying to connect, recoiling from hurt and reaching toward love. Every person deserves to be surrounded by positive, kind and supportive people—especially you!

Questions for Exploration: **HEALTHY RELATIONSHIPS**

• Do the people closest to you add light to your life? Do they have a positive effect on you? Do they want what is truly best for you?

• Do you feel emotionally and physically safe with your friends? With your spouse or partner?

• Are you fearful, anxious, or extremely unhappy in your current relationship? Do you feel it may be in your best interest to let go of that relationship and move forward?

• What are your expectations of healthy friends, partners, family members, co-workers, and bosses? What defines a healthy relationship to you?

• What does the principle of trust mean to you?

• How are your communication skills? What could you do to improve communication in your life?

• Do you give more than you take? Take more than you give? What can you do to come into balance?

• If you are struggling to let go of toxic relationships, what support can you get to help you through the transition?

Chapter 8

GRATITUDE

"There are only two ways to live your life. One is as though nothing is a miracle. The other is as if everything is."

—ALBERT EINSTEIN

"If you've forgotten the language of gratitude, you'll never be on speaking terms with happiness."

—OLD PROVERB

When we talk about rewiring the brain for joy, serenity, and sobriety, nothing is as effective as the healing emotion of gratitude. Gratitude both grounds us in the present moment and connects us to those around us. It is the practice of thankfulness—counting one's blessings as they unfold each day and cultivating a perspective on life that focuses solely on the positive.

According to research studies conducted at the National Institute of Health, hypothalamus activity in the brain during meditations on gratitude was observed at record high levels. The hypothalamus controls stress levels, metabolism, sleep cycles, and emotional stability, all of which were improved when subjects ruminated on the good in their lives. Furthermore, brain regions related to the "feel-good" neurotransmitter dopamine were charged and activated, revealing gratitude as a natural anti-depressant. Dopamine's chemical powers also reward the reinforcement of patterns; therefore, the repetition of thankfulness actually perpetuates more of the same emotion, changing your perception of reality.

The NIH was not the only facility to make these observations. At Eastern Washington University, psychologist Philip Watkins measured the gratitude levels of a depressed population and found them to be nearly twice as low as those of a healthy control group. Neuropsychologists at the Greater Good Science Center have also linked gratitude to physical advantages such as a stronger immune response and lower blood pressure. In addition, researchers have found that gratitude is the bedrock of happy marriages, successful business partnerships, and indeed all stable, fulfilling relationships in life.

Gratitude is a state of mind, an insistence on a certain perspective that accentuates and affirms life while rejecting negativity. One of the most poignant examples of this perspective came from a member of the Innocence Project, an organization that works to exonerate people on death row who have been proven innocent through previously unavailable DNA sampling. These men and women had been wrongly imprisoned, some for as long as 20 years. One particular man was asked whether he was bitter. Unbelievably, he replied, "What would be the point? I only have so much time on Earth and I want to make the most of my freedom from this point forward." His bravery in setting aside the tragedy of so many lost years is an inspiration to us all. Gratitude helps us to forgive the unforgiveable, to heal the gravest of injustices. By choosing to live in the present moment, rather than dwell on the unchangeable past, we can avoid losing more precious time, of which so much has already been sacrificed to addiction.

LEARNING TO BE GRATEFUL

Gratitude is not a popular trend in our capitalist society. If we're grateful for what we have, then we can't be constantly sold products and services that cater to our insecurities and our desire to outdo the Joneses. Everywhere we look we are bombarded by the idea that we need to be richer, thinner, smarter, funnier, more charming, and, of course, better looking. If we liked ourselves just the way we are the advertising industry would tank—and they know it.

Yes, it's true; there will always be people who are more attractive than us, more accomplished, and more intelligent. There will *also* always be folks that are less so. Learning to appreciate the good in everyone and seeing ourselves as connected to others helps us to be content with our place in the world, knowing that we are neither more nor less valuable than anyone else. When one man goes to the moon, we all rejoice. "Look at what our species can do!" We can enjoy each person we meet as a reflection of the infinite variations of humanity, knowing that, just as an orchestra would be incomplete without the tuba, the piccolo, or the timpani, so would mankind be less rich if any one of us was missing. Instead of striving to be perfect, we should just marvel at our good fortune to be here at all. As they say, it sure beats the alternative!

Real Recovery: Julie

When I first started to incorporate the principle of gratitude in my practice, I came across a patient named Julie. She was given everything as a child; some would even call her spoiled. Yet although she lacked for nothing in the material realm, her basic approach to life centered on a sense of entitlement, which only grew stronger over the years. Entitlement is the belief that life owes you the things you want and feel you deserve. It's a corrosive force that eats away at happiness and serenity. Through my sessions with Julie, I gradually learned that, although Julie's parents loved her and showered her with possessions, she had never felt cared for emotionally or valued for her authentic self. She resented her mom and dad for their neglect, and as a teenager with nowhere to turn when she was sad, angry, or frustrated, she started using alcohol and drugs to fill the void.

When I began working with Julie, she was very resistant to the concept of gratitude; she had no idea what it meant to count her blessings. She was unaware that, even though life is hard at times, there is always someone out there who has it worse. Gradually, Julie started to let go of her preconceptions of how things "should" be and began to appreciate the positives in her life. She learned to communicate with her parents about what she needed, being sure to also bless them for providing all that they had. She became more positive, and expressed gratitude for her health, the roof over her head, and her friends and family. Her grades went back up and today she is substance-free and attending college. Julie is a miracle of shifting perception and proof that there is no medicine quite like gratitude.

FINDING A PLACE FOR GRATITUDE

During my own drinking days, I too took for granted the people and comforts that I had in my life when I was younger. I thought my family's concerns and warnings about my health were just plain nagging. I was frustrated and annoyed by their constant concern for my well being. I began to harbor more and more secrets. My mom's incessant preaching and paranoia was just chatter to me. I completely disregarded anything she had to say. I knew better, after all; I knew what was best for me.

How wrong I was! Not only did I lack gratitude for my family's concern, I also had no appreciation for my health. I knew very well that drinking and staying up all night at bars and parties was not good for my mind, body, or spirit. I took for granted that my body would recuperate and heal. All while knowing that, when it did, I would destroy it again with the ethanol poison.

It was not until I stopped drinking and started applying these principles to my life that I really understood what gratitude was. I was so grateful for a second chance at life, an opportunity to live with the blinders off, feeling the simple warmth of the sun. I wanted to be front and center to experience it *all*—beauty, joy, sadness, ugliness, suffering, success, grief, and so much more. I was finally awake to the rainbow of emotions and the continuum of the human experience.

I began to count my blessings daily. I would think at least once a day about the blessings I had. I had my eyes to see, my lungs to breathe, as every organ in my body was working, pumping blood to my heart and brain. I was grateful for my books to read, the roof over my head, my wonderful family, friends, lovers, and every human that had ever loved me and whom I ever loved.

And as I thought about this daily, I began to develop a habit where, when I had come to the end of my run in the morning, I would pause the music blasting in my ears and take off my headphones. I would look up at the trees, sky, and sun. I would take in what a blessing this day is. I would then thank God for my health, sobriety, family, and the love in my life. And I wouldn't just say it, but *feel* it in the depths of my being and soul. I still try to do this daily, even though I can't always do it perfectly. None of us are perfect, but we can still find a way to incorporate gratitude into our lives daily.

GRATITUDE FROM A TO Z

One of the tools I use to help clients ease into the habit of experiencing authentic gratitude is a game called "Thank You A to Z." It's kind of like a kid's game, in the way it can jolt your mind into playfulness and curiosity, especially when you are feeling prone to negative emotions such as self-pity, victimhood, and perpetual "not-enoughness." These are very human emotions that we all encounter, but it's what we choose to do about them that counts.

You can play this game all day long, wherever you go. Just look around and find something that starts with "A" to be grateful for. Apples, Air, Arias, Amour, Ansel Adams! Then, proceed through the alphabet: Berries, Bowling, Beethoven, Breath, Bulldogs! By naming all the things you cherish and adore in this life, you cannot help but walk away with renewed joy and relief. Finally, you can be free from comparing yourself to others and coming up short; nothing is more draining than focusing on what we lack.

You can use a similar gratitude game to create a "Celebrating Me" day for just yourself. Start with your body. What do you appreciate about it? Do you enjoy walking, breathing, listening, seeing, tasting, and smelling? Thank the universe for these bounties. The human body, with all its complex systems, is nothing short of a miracle. If you've ever met someone for whom one of these vital functions is compromised, then you probably have some idea as to how lucky you are to have a body that works on its own and is relatively healthy.

So it goes with the mind. Most of us take it for granted that we can think and calculate and make sense of our experiences. Schizophrenics and others with severe mental illnesses have no such ease. Make a list of all the ways your mind works to protect you. Every mechanism in the mind and body is wired for self-protection; for instance, if you clam up before giving a speech, instead of being angry or ashamed you can say, "Thank you for warning me of danger, dear hormones." Even addiction itself is something to be grateful for. The numbness it provided through adolescence or other difficult years may have saved your life.

Another great way to show gratitude is to go on a 30-day generosity binge. These gifts need not be extravagant; on the contrary, a gift can be as simple as a compliment to a stranger, a phone call to a sick friend, a dollar stuck in a homeless man's jar, or a few minutes spent helping a relative change a tire. Doing these kinds of selfless actions every day can yield amazing breakthroughs, as you become aware of your own power to bring happiness to others; to sooth and cheer; to alleviate others of doubt, sadness, and loneliness.

Along these lines, there are hundreds of opportunities to be of service to your community through volunteer work, mentoring and resource-sharing. Teaching incarcerated men and women to read and write, using your business skills to coach young people just starting out, or answering calls at a suicide prevention hotline—these kinds of commitments teach us how vulnerable others can be, and how much we have to contribute to the greater healing process on this earth. Each of us has so much to offer, and as we begin to own up to our talents, knowledge, and experience, we find that once-habitual sense of discontentment slips away, replaced with a feeling of real purpose. Gratitude is truly an action—a living prayer.

Gratitude also allows us to turn misfortune into fortune, and victimhood into survivorship. Once we grasp the idea that we are not alone in our pain, whatever it may be, we can start using our traumatic pasts to offer others a way out—serving as a torch through the darkness. This can range from writing a book about one's experience to starting a foundation or becoming a professional healer. Seeing how our experiences can benefit others is the key to eliminating the remorse that often accompanies our first period of sobriety. If we don't choose to use our pain constructively, it can lead us down the path of "What's the use?" and endanger all the hard work we've done to get clean.

Just for today, try to find one thing to be grateful for. You may be miserable, but try to find out which part of that misery comes from a limited, faulty perspective. A wise person once remarked that there are two types of fears: that of not getting what you want and that of losing what you already have. Gratitude is the solution to both. It's very difficult to attract more good into your life if you are busy meditating on what you don't yet have. If you are angry and bitter now, you will only be more angry and bitter when you have more; it will never be enough to fill that empty hole inside.

Instead, we have to start with where we are today. Do you have a roof over your head? Food to eat? Clothing? Someone to talk to? A special animal companion? Those are all treasures to cherish. One day all your dreams may come true, but as long as you are in the habit of finding the flaws in everything and everyone, you won't be present to receive such miracles. You will be busy obsessing over the next conquest or acquisition, or bemoaning the most recent defeat or loss. So, just for today, enjoy what you *do* have and make an effort to brighten someone else's day.

Questions for Exploration: **GRATITUDE**

- What are you grateful for?

- Do you have a sense of entitlement?

- Do you engage in self-pity?

- Do you feel lucky to be you? Why or why not?

- How often do you compare yourself to others?

- Do you buy into advertising messages about your self-worth?

- What steps can you take to celebrate yourself?

- What painful experiences are you grateful for? What have you learned and how have you grown?

- How can you show others you are grateful for them today?

- How can you give back to your community, your family, and those who have supported you during your struggles with active addiction?

Chapter 9

COMPASSION

"Too often we underestimate the power of a touch, a smile, a kind word, a listening ear, an honest compliment, or the smallest act of caring, all of which have the potential to turn a life around."

—Leo Buscaglia

ynthia was bullied as a child. Her father was in the military, so her family was always moving. Each time she attended a new school, she'd get teased about her weight and appearance. As much as she tried to fit in, she always failed, which led to low self-esteem and doubts about her self worth. She believed these bullies when they told her she was a loser. Gradually, these voices telling her she would never amount to anything became internalized—her peers' negative comments had bled into her own self-talk.

In high school, she found a group of friends who partied, smoked weed, cut school, and were labeled "the outcasts." She finally felt like she belonged. Using drugs and alcohol numbed her insecurities, and she quickly learned how to drown out the negative voices.

When I met Cynthia, I asked her to name three things she liked about herself. She could not think of one. I knew right then that we had to nurture the wounded child within her, and that the best way to do so was by teaching her the principle of compassion. As we started working with affirmations about kindness to self and others, Cynthia began to see her value, worth, and beauty as a human being. That negative voice slowly dissipated, and she did not need the partying and using to check out anymore. She praised herself for what she had accomplished and who she was. Compassion was her path toward sobriety, and through it she finally found the peace and connection that had eluded her for so long.

So often as addicts we harbor deep childhood wounds that, while invisible, affect our thoughts and actions on a daily basis. We may be surrounded by loving friends, counselors, partners, and family members, but their praise and affection does nothing to penetrate the force field of self-loathing that keeps us in pain. Facing the emotional memories of cruelty and neglect can be a challenge unless we can cultivate a sense of compassion. How can we do this, though, if we've never experienced it?

WHAT IS COMPASSION?

The dictionary defines compassion along the lines of empathy: "A feeling of deep sympathy and sorrow for another who is stricken by misfortune, accompanied by a strong desire to alleviate the suffering." Compassion is unconditional. We don't just feel it for some; we feel it for all living things. For some of us, it's actually easier to express compassion for others than it is for ourselves. We can use this to our benefit, asking, "Would I call my friend these awful names I call myself? Or put them down when they need my support most? Would I chastise my friend, pointing out their flaws until they felt like crying?" Perhaps we have felt empathy for an abandoned kitten, or a stranger who crossed our path, or maybe even for a fictional character in a movie. But if we can reach somewhere inside ourselves and access the spirit of kindness, we can build upon it—even if it feels false at first. When we hear hurtful messages running through our heads, we can catch ourselves and learn to disagree. Compassion is self-acceptance and acceptance of others. It means an end to demands, comparisons, and complaints. We are all flawed, and compassion teaches us that despite this, we still very much deserve love.

Compassion was something that was foreign to me when I began my recovery. I was hurting myself physically, emotionally, and mentally with ethanol poison, using a substance to numb my anxiety. I was deeply uncomfortable in my own skin, and I was filled with shame and loneliness. My true self began to whisper to me, "You know you deserve more in this life. You are destined to find love and happiness, and to help others." I knew this deep in my soul. Yet the more I considered how serious my addiction had become, the more I felt the need to drown out that true self voice with poison. It was an endless cycle. What I didn't understand at the time was that in order to end this suffering, I had to turn and run headlong into the arms of compassion.

Finally, my mother picked me up one day. She was crying. She said to me, "Erica, I love you and want you to have happiness back in your life. You are a most wonderful person, and I am so upset that you cannot help yourself. Please let me help you." I was lucky to have my mother intervene like that. She had tried so many times in the past, but I would always make up an excuse as to why I was missing, not answering calls, or shaking. I would deny, deny, deny. But this time was different. My true self's whisper was louder than my addict self's voice. I finally broke down and let her help me. That was when I went into treatment, and it saved my life. I had to be physically removed from San Francisco, my environment, and be put somewhere safe. Then I began to learn.

Gradually, my heart and mind began to open as I found out I was not alone. I ran quickly toward compassion. I knew I would have to start building that muscle. I began to speak to myself nicely. I would congratulate myself when I would work out, take a bath, or get in bed early. I would literally pat myself on the shoulder and call myself sweet names. I had to develop that kind of self love and care. I did that daily. I made it part of my plan and took an oath to say one compassionate or nice thing to myself every day. It changed my life. I still struggle as we all do, but I treat myself with care and compassion, first and foremost.

LEARNING COMPASSION THROUGH AFFIRMATIONS

One of the best methods of silencing the hateful voices in our heads is to work with affirmations, especially guided meditations that can be listened to aloud. The gentle words of a healer can land deeply within our consciousness and replace the voices of those that damaged us. Over time, we can't help but believe the new messages we are absorbing.

Looking into the mirror and reciting affirmations is likewise highly effective. Making eye contact with yourself and expressing love, appreciation, and respect may strike some as corny or over-the-top, but if that is your reaction, perhaps it's time to give it a try. People who love themselves unconditionally can express self-love without making a joke out of it.

Another extremely useful exercise I developed to help clients is called the Compliment Log. It's a small journal you carry with you to record every nice thing that others say about you. Being smiled at, invited out, hugged or otherwise included/embraced also counts. If you do this consistently, you will be amazed by the changes in your perception. Suddenly, you may find the world full of benevolence rather than hostility. You will begin to accept your own wonderfulness and *own* it, no longer able to deny the evidence before you, all of which is attesting to your true value.

COMPASSION TOWARD OTHERS

Once we are easier on ourselves, we can start to give others a break, too. If someone offends us, we can pause before rushing to judgment, giving them the benefit of the doubt. One of the chief ways we can begin to incorporate compassion into our recovery is to practice "verbal harmlessness." This means abstaining from such soul-crushers as gossip, negativity, and character assassination. In the Buddhist tradition, the principle of compassion is an indispensable pillar of enlightenment. At its root is the dissolution of separateness between ourselves and others. The Golden Rule of treating others as we would like to be treated becomes effortless, because we no longer differentiate between ourselves and others. *Metta*, or loving-kindness, incorporates the practices of friendliness, benevolence, amity, good will, being on the same mental wavelength, and having an active interest in others. Sometimes having compassion can be as simple as asking a customer service professional how their day is going, or acknowledging a person whom you see often but never speak to. Choosing to focus on what's best in other people can actually increase our serenity and happiness, which in turn fortifies our sobriety.

FORGIVENESS

If all this talk of kindness and compassion makes your blood boil, perhaps it is time to look toward the principle of forgiveness. In some ways, forgiveness is a prerequisite for compassion. Letting go of the past and releasing the heavy grudges we harbor toward others can be an intense and cleansing ritual. Our resentments may be fully justified, but the energy we spend tied up in knots over another's behavior cripples us. It holds us back from enjoying the levity and lack of drama that are compassion's natural by-products.

Forgiveness can be thought of as having three directions, or three viewpoints. We first contemplate the harms *we* have done, admitting that there are many ways we have hurt others. In doing so, we forgive ourselves. For an addict, the shame and guilt associated with prior behavior can become a constant source of suffering and can lead down the dangerous path of self-medication through relapse. We may feel the desire to mercilessly turn the screws, wallowing in remorse and self-pity over our misdeeds, but instead we should treat ourselves with simple kindness as we would a young child who made a mistake.

Secondly, we contemplate the harms we've done to *ourselves*. We may have abandoned ourselves, maimed our bodies with food, drugs or alcohol, exposed ourselves to untold dangers and sordid company, but we must find the compassion to forgive these mistakes as well. We make the mental and spiritual choice to accept our own apology.

Lastly, we explore the harms *others* have done to us. We summon the principle of tolerance, no matter how distasteful a pill it may be to swallow. We accept that we do not know the whole story about the people who hurt us. We may feel that justice has not been served, or that these so-called enemies should be punished, but we have no idea as to the quality of their internal lives or the amount of pain that may have driven them to lash out at others in the first place.

SURROUNDING OURSELVES WITH COMPASSION

Sometimes we need to acknowledge that our relationships with other people mirror the ones we have with ourselves. In certain cases, we may need to take some responsibility for engaging with those we are angry at in the first place. If we continuously find ourselves attracted to someone who is unkind, we may need to examine whether that person is merely vocalizing aloud a lot of the beliefs we ourselves hold within.

In the end, we may simply need to bless these offending parties, accepting that we may never truly understand why they acted as they did. The resolution and closure we seek may only be possible within our own mind and heart, and through forgiveness we can finally close the chapter on the part they played in our lives. To forgive someone who harmed you gravely is perhaps one of the hardest steps you will ever have to take in recovery. It goes against all the cells in our bodies that scream out to "get even." It may plunge us into a world of grief, but as we move through it, we enter into a life of pleasure, ease, and true joy. No longer burdened by the heaviness of our grudges, we find lasting sobriety and wholeness. To bear witness to this cleansing process, we may want to enact a ritual such as writing down the events, people, places, or emotions from our past that still haunt us, and finish by burning the list, releasing the ashes to the winds and finally letting go.

As with all the principles in this book, compassion can be learned, and according to research studies at the University of Wisconsin-Madison, it can be learned in the same way as an instrument, a sport, or a language. No matter how damaged or incapable we may feel, the truth is that we can be reprogrammed. The fact that the brain is softwired rather than hardwired means that there is hope for everyone to change, from the most hardened criminal to the most ruthless dictator. If we can wrap our minds around this truth, we can go a long way toward helping ourselves to withhold final judgment on others.

Kindness begins to feel wonderful as we come to practice forgiveness without a second thought. In fact, there is evidence to suggest that meditating on compassion actually increases the happy chemicals in our brains. Scientists at Emory University have even showed that compassion reduces stress and boosts the immune system. Participants were divided into two groups and those who spent six weeks meditating on compassion showed around 50 percent lower levels of stress than their non-meditating counterparts. As addicts, we can't afford to ignore these numbers. Stress is a powerful trigger that has led many an alcoholic and drug user back to slavery.

As you read this chapter and work on the study questions, I would invite you to start small. Find one way to forgive yourself today, and then find one other person to forgive. Choose one affirmation from Chapter 11 and say it to yourself in the mirror. Finally, choose one thing you like about yourself—physical, mental, emotional, or spiritual—and draw a picture of it. Place this drawing someplace where you can look at it every day and remember that this is the beginning of a very beautiful friendship!

Questions for Exploration: COMPASSION

- Do you find being compassionate toward yourself easy?
- Do you feel guilty or ashamed of who you are or your actions?
- In what areas do you need to practice self-acceptance?
- In what ways do you need to be more accepting of others?
- Where and when can you give others the benefit of the doubt?
- Do you practice relative ethics, treating some people well and others not so well?
- What does tolerance mean to you? Do you practice it?
- Do you have anger issues? How can the principle of compassion help you to manage your rage?
- How well do you give and receive compliments?
- Do you forgive easily?
- Have you been holding a grudge?
- What would it mean to forgive everyone in your life? What would it feel like?
- How has shame and guilt driven your addiction?
- What would it feel like to be free from all shame and guilt?

Chapter 10

LOVE

"I define love: The will to extend one's self for the purpose of nurturing one's own or another's spiritual growth."

—M. Scott Peck

"There are two basic motivating forces: fear and love. When we are afraid, we pull back from life. When we are in love, we open to all that life has to offer with passion, excitement, and acceptance. We need to learn to love ourselves first, in all our glory and our imperfections. If we cannot love ourselves, we cannot fully open to our ability to love others or our potential to create. Evolution and all hopes for a better world rest in the fearlessness and open-hearted vision of people who embrace life."

—John Lennon

Since time immemorial, poets, gurus, and philosophers have toiled to define the most potent and indispensable word in the human language—love. Some have heralded it as the force that makes the world go 'round. Others have described it in terms of the pain it can cause when it's not returned. It's been used to denote the feeling a mother has for her child; that which Mother Teresa felt for the poor; that a lover has for their beloved. In truth, love is a word that encompasses all the other principles discussed in this book. It is the crowning jewel of all the work you have done on your recovery so far. Love contains within it the ability to be authentic and honest; to enforce healthy boundaries in relationships; to be grateful and compassionate. The ability to evolve, manage one's time, engage in solitude and practice self-care are all components of love. Every person on Earth, from infancy to old age, needs love. Love is the sunlight of the soul that allows us to grow, flower, and produce the fruits of our imaginations. Love is the life force of our spirit. Love is also a magnetic force. The more love we give, the more love we draw to us.

OVERCOMING FEAR AND FINDING LOVE

Like sunlight, love comes with its own shadow—fear. It drives us to doubt our hearts, to avoid risks, to labor at "secure" jobs or marry partners who don't ignite our passion—in other words, to play it safe. Fear drives us to pretend that love is foolish and a waste of time. It fills us with jealousy, possessiveness, and the need to control things—all forces that *repel* love rather than foster it. Underneath fear lies the knowledge that as human beings, we can never be entirely self-sufficient. We are designed to be interdependent, not isolated islands. The very fact that we were born helpless, in dire need of warmth, kindness, food, touch, and shelter makes us vulnerable in a way that many other animals are not. The human baby will require intense care and protection for many years as it develops physically, mentally, and emotionally. When these needs fail to be met and love is withheld, we may develop the erroneous idea that our own dependency is to blame. We then withdraw from intimacy of all kinds, and many of us never find the courage to return.

Where love is lacking, trauma is most often to blame, and at the root of trauma is a betrayal of love. For some of us it might have happened at age 3, for others at age 30, but somewhere along the line, we had an experience that cut us off from the sunlight of the soul. Like a tree falling across the road, we allowed this event to derail us from our path in life, embarking on the dead-end detour of addiction. We may have loved our families, but instead of loving us back, they abused us. We may have been in love with another person, and instead of being embraced, we were rejected. For some, our love manifested as a career dream that somehow slipped through our fingers. Regardless of the individual circumstances, we allowed fear to keep us from ever trying to connect again. We shut down and tuned out, content to drink or drug ourselves into oblivion and eventual death. Learning to love again after we have been hurt, however, is the defining moment in every addict's recovery—the make-it-or-break-it decision that will determine what kind of future we will have in this life. Fortunately, we face this decision every day—there is literally a continuous stream of opportunities to choose love over fear.

The secret truth is that love is abundant; it is not scarce. Our trauma may have convinced us that love was a rare, impossible entity, a certain kind of light that would never shine on us, but this is just distorted thinking based on our subjective, negative experiences. There is a Winnie the Pooh illustration of Eeyore the gloomy donkey walking around with a rain cloud over him. Everywhere else, the sun is shining—except for over Eeyore's head, so he mistakenly believes that the weather is always bad. It is similar for those of us who come from trauma. Our entire life view is veiled with the fog of mistrust and cynicism. We just are not aware of how much love awaits us once we open ourselves to receiving it. Everywhere on this earth there are people working for the good of humanity, laboring to bring freedom, happiness, and security to their fellows. We may never see this on the mainstream media channels, as positive news does not often qualify as "news" at all, but behind the scenes there are scores of benevolent people who wish us well. Chances are that if you are in recovery, you may have encountered a few of these kind strangers. They are the ones who save our lives at the hospital when we almost overdose; they man the suicide hotlines into the wee hours of the morning; they are the ones who sit with us week after week in counseling sessions listening to and understanding us; they are all the people who worked to make this book possible. You may not believe it right away, but you are always loved and supported.

Real Recovery: Jake

Jake was a star football player in high school, with a bright future as a college athlete. But during his senior year, as the pressure to succeed mounted, he became involved with meth and crack, which quickly stripped him of all ambition, passion, and his desire to pursue sports. Within less than a year, his debilitating addiction had left him home-less, living on the floor of a recording studio.

Jake became my client while in rehab. After hearing his story, I crafted a recovery plan that included all the elements discussed so far in this book which, when added together, amounted to what Jake was sorely missing the most: love. He needed to learn *how* to love himself, through evolution, gratitude, self-care, compassion, honesty, authentic-ity, time management, and by seeking out healthy solitude and healthy relationships. He needed to remember that it was love that made him pursue football in the first place.

In his first weeks of being clean, he developed a routine to make sure he got enough sleep. He slowly began training again. Little by little, he rediscovered the love of playing football, which had once been at the center of his life. Soon his dream was back on track; from there, he quickly made huge leaps and strides toward a complete recovery from drug addition. He enrolled at a community college and is now a quarterback for his team. These days, he is motivated by his love of the game, rather than the need to win. He now plans to transfer to a four-year university. Jake is truly a leader and an inspiration to others; his self-love and self-respect allowed him to regain his lost opportunities and become the person he wanted to be.

FINDING LOVE IN OUR LIVES

To venture beyond mere survival and learn to thrive in sobriety requires a decision to believe in love and to accept it, even when it doesn't come from traditional sources. Because we are conditioned to desire love chiefly from our nuclear families or a romantic partner, we may sometimes turn our noses up at love from other channels, just as a body might reject an organ transplant. Once we affirm that love is love, regardless of its source, we can begin feeling its warmth all around us in unexpected, exciting ways. One of the best exercises in this vein is to focus on what you have in common with people rather than on the differences. When you walk into a party, a club, a concert, or a football game and you feel alone, you can either think, "All these people hate me. I am so different," or you can think, "We all love dancing/music/football! We are very similar."

The love you have in common with others is a wonderful starting point for a feeling of connection. Maybe you're walking into a business meeting or a job interview. You can direct your thoughts toward the common ground you share with the authority figures. After all, you've both chosen the same field in life, so you are kindred spirits of a kind. In this way, love becomes a practical tool you can use to navigate potentially tense or alienating situations.

If we're truly at a loss for incoming love, we can always focus on the love we have to give. Strangely enough, expressing love toward others has the same affect as receiving love. To express love is a human freedom that can never be taken away, no matter the circumstances. Even in prison, there are always people who choose to spend their time creating art, taking classes, and teaching a skill to fellow inmates, while others become mired in power struggles, addiction, and negativity. During the Holocaust, there were always those men and women in the prison camps who went around giving away their last crust of bread to someone more needy, or taking the time to tell stories that might cheer up their friends. Living in love is a choice.

In my life, love was something I always had. I was the first-born child for my parents, the first grandchild and the first niece on both sides of my family, so I received a lot of attention and affection. It is what I believe gave me a second chance to live this life of sobriety, truth, and health. I lost that briefly during the years that I suffered with alcohol addiction. I took love for granted. I stopped loving myself, and I almost gave up entirely on romantic love once or twice. But as soon as I quit abusing the substance, I began to know real compassion for myself and others. I began living my truth. Love returned to my life. It even started to grow and multiply into a kind of love I had never experienced.

When you give yourself the gift of being truly present in your life, love can show up in a most dazzling way. It is what keeps you going, and it is the ultimate reward you can give and receive, so be grateful for every act of love you encounter.

Questions for Exploration: LOVE

- How do you see love manifesting in your life?
- In what ways have you chosen love over fear?
- In what ways have you yet to do so?
- In what ways do you practice self-love?
- Is it easier to say something nice to someone else, but harder to say it to your own self?
- How do you show your love toward family and friends? Toward your partner?
- How do you cope with jealousy?
- Have you experienced a significant loss of love?
- What can you do to open your heart once more?

Chapter 11

AFFIRMATIONS AND INTENTIONS

"Today is the day for you to begin creating a joyous, fulfilling life. Today is the day to begin to release all your limitations. Today is the day for you to learn the secrets of life. You can change your life for the better. You already have the tools within you to do so. These tools are your thoughts and your beliefs."

—LOUISE HAY

The idea that words contain a magical power has held great importance in innumerable cultures throughout history. The ancient Hindus, Sikhs and Buddhists used mantras, or "sacred speech," to harness their spiritual and psychic powers. In modern traditions, a magician in Las Vegas might say the word, "Abracadabra!" when pulling a rabbit out of thin air or making one disappear. The spectacle may seem comical and superficial, but the word "Abracadabra" is derived from the Aramaic phrase *avra kehdabra*, meaning, "I will create as I speak." This is exactly what we do when we choose to perform an affirmation. We conjure up an ideal to aspire to, and with repetition, this ideal becomes our new reality. It is a magical and transformative act.

Affirmations help us to cope with any situation, no matter how challenging. They rewire our brains to see opportunities rather than disasters, successes rather than failures, and positive attributes rather than negative ones. The concept in itself seems like a hoax. How can I honestly say that things are good when I feel they are bad? The answer to this question can be seen very clearly in how our body reacts when using muscle memory. For example, if you go to memorize lyrics to your favorite song, you may not sing it exactly right the first time through. But the more that you practice, the more you are automatically able to sing along with utter confidence. Your brain becomes accustomed to repeating that same task until it decides that it is more efficient to just do it spontaneously.

I highly recommend practicing some sort of meditation, visualization, or positive affirmation first thing in the morning when you wake up. Remember that many of your first thoughts affect how you will live the rest of your day. The more you use affirmations, the stronger and quicker you will see the results materialize in your life. Try to visualize an outcome you would like to manifest. Try to picture what it would look like, how it would feel, sound, and even smell. Breathe in and imagine how you want your life to look; capture that feeling with all your senses.

To assist you, let's take a look at some positive affirmations we can use to rewire our brains into adapting to change, rather than resisting it.

AFFIRMATIONS ON AUTHENTICITY

Today I will remain true to myself. I will honor my feelings.

I say what I mean and mean what I say.

I release the need to wear masks.

I am loved for being exactly the way I am.

The more I follow my own heart, the more others love and respect me.

I let go of the need to people-please.

It is safe to speak my truth.

I have the right to be inconsistent.

I have the right to take my time.

I have the right to take space from others when I need it.

I have the right to take a different path.

I am unique in all the world.

My work reflects my deepest joy.

My relationships reflect my true values.

My actions and values are harmoniously aligned.

I surround myself with people who support my authentic self.

I honor my inner voice unconditionally.

I am connected firmly and passionately to my true self.

I accept myself.

I allow others to see and know the real me.

AFFIRMATIONS ON HONESTY

My soul heals through honesty and truthfulness.

I am an honest person.

I always tell the truth.

I am known as a truthful, trustworthy individual.

I find it easy to admit my mistakes.

I tell the truth even when it is inconvenient.

I tell the truth even when it is embarrassing.

I tell the truth even when I fear the repercussions.

I keep my promises.

I strive for accuracy.

I let go of the need to minimize or exaggerate.

I trust that there are always solutions to my problems.

I can get my needs met without lying.

I am emotionally honest.

I acknowledge my abilities and strengths.

I live in enduring integrity.

I do not steal or cheat.

The more honest I am, the more intimacy I experience with others.

I face everything and recover.

When I give my word, it means something.

AFFIRMATIONS ON EVOLUTION

It is safe to shine.

I realize my potential, and I honor it.

I allow myself to be in a process.

I value the journey as much as the destination.

I release my perfectionism and move forward without fear.

It's okay to make mistakes.

I have the courage to follow my dreams.

I have a bright future.

I love trying new things.

I enjoy taking risks and stepping outside my comfort zone.

I own all my talents and abilities.

I embrace the beginner's mind.

I cultivate new hobbies that I enjoy.

It is okay to be a late bloomer.

I am in the right place at the right time doing the right thing.

I seek out positive role models and mentors.

I enjoy meeting new people and new people enjoy meeting me.

Happy, loving people are eager to meet me.

I reward myself for a job well done.

I accept praise and appreciation for my work.

AFFIRMATIONS ON SOLITUDE

I enjoy my own company.

I am my own best friend.

I spend some time alone every day.

I am responsible for my own happiness.

It is safe to put myself first.

I enjoy connecting with nature.

I thrive on my own validation.

I make time for relaxation, meditation, and adequate sleep.

I practice healthy boundaries in all my relationships.

I cultivate an inner sanctuary of peace and serenity.

I take myself on great dates.

I am grounded in my senses and in the present moment.

I enjoy reading and cultivating new hobbies.

I enjoy getting to know myself better.

I release the need for drama and chaos in my life.

I find joy in the simple things in life.

I use my solitude as another channel for self-discovery.

I experience solitude as a wonderful adventure.

I enjoy the silence of my own mind.

I am comfortable with myself.

AFFIRMATIONS ON TIME MANAGEMENT

I am at peace with time.

I set boundaries with ease.

I have plenty of time for each task I need to perform today.

I love being productive.

I am in the right place at the right time doing the right thing.

I have enough time, enough love, and enough money.

I find safe harbor in the present moment.

I allow myself to spend time doing nothing.

I release the need for chaos around time.

I release the need to procrastinate.

I release the need for chronic tardiness.

I give myself enough time to get where I need to go.

I create a schedule of balance and harmony.

Self-care takes the highest priority in my schedule.

Every day I take time to nurture my creative visions.

I reward myself for time well spent.

Beginning today, what serves me stays and what fails me goes.

Time is a valuable resource that I will spend wisely.

I am careful to balance work with play and socializing with solitude.

I have all the time in the world and everything I need.

AFFIRMATIONS ON SELF-CARE

Today I will take responsibility for my life, my health, and my happiness.

I love myself unconditionally.

I allow myself the proper amount of food, sleep, and enjoyment each day.

I am worthy.

I am beautiful.

I am perfect just as I am.

I am free from negative substances, people, and energy.

I find time to exercise every week.

I nourish my mind and my spirit on a regular basis.

Each day I do one thing to develop my intellect.

I take time to discover what is spiritual for me.

I allow myself to experience and express emotions with ease.

The more I love myself, the more others love me.

When I am troubled, I pause to comfort myself and understand my feelings.

I nourish my body with healthy food every day.

I enjoy giving to myself as much as others.

I accept the things I cannot change.

I am strong physically, mentally, and emotionally.

Today is my day. There is no person, no thing, no event or activity that can destroy this day for me.

Today is the first day of the rest of my life and I will take notice of the many positive things this day has to offer.

AFFIRMATIONS ON HEALTHY RELATIONSHIPS

I am drawing healthy, loving people into my life one day at a time.

I am honest, trustworthy, and kind.

I am reliable and helpful.

I accept others as they are without trying to change them.

I acknowledge my needs and communicate them clearly to others.

I deserve to be loved and liked.

I treat others the way I enjoy being treated.

My heart is open, and I am surrounded by people who support me.

My relationships nurture my recovery.

My partner is generous and kind.

I only attract positive people into my life.

My relationships are grounded in integrity.

I am safe and well-treated.

I have the right to be treated with respect.

I excel at setting boundaries.

I achieve the perfect balance between self-care and time spent with others.

I let go of toxic relationships.

I detach with love.

I enjoy meeting new people and new people enjoy meeting me.

I am loved for being exactly the way I am.

AFFIRMATIONS ON GRATITUDE

Every day I appreciate my life more than ever.

Every day I give thanks for all that blesses my life.

Mistakes are learning experiences that help me grow.

With every breath I take, I am bringing more and more gratitude into my life.

Through the continuous expression of gratitude, I am now living a life of unlimited abundance.

My grateful heart attracts more of everything I appreciate in life.

I treat life as the ultimate gift.

I sincerely appreciate the support I receive from others.

I take the time to appreciate the simple things in life.

I thank people often.

I pay my bills with gratitude.

I gratefully accept all the good that manifests in my life.

I am very grateful that I am able to reprogram my life for the better.

I appreciate all forms of life on this planet.

I focus on what I have, what I can give, and what I love.

I honor all that is good about me.

I own everything about myself.

I am grateful for my past and use it to uplift others.

I am grateful for my body, mind, and spirit.

Through gratitude, I move from surviving to thriving.

AFFIRMATIONS ON COMPASSION

I am non-judgmental and forgiving.

I forgive myself and others with ease.

I accept mistakes as part of being human.

I am kind and gentle toward everyone I meet.

I see what I can do to contribute.

I am generous and loving toward myself and others.

I release the need to bully myself or others.

I let go of shame and guilt.

I use positive language and verbal harmlessness.

I abstain from gossip and character assassination.

I give and receive compliments with ease.

I give others the benefit of the doubt.

Easy does it.

I am friendly.

I take an active interest in others.

I take the time to put a smile on another person's face.

I do what I can to help those less fortunate than me.

I let go of grudges and focus on the here and now.

I let go of the past and live in the present moment.

I am positive, connected, and I express love with ease.

AFFIRMATIONS ON LOVE

I am deserving of love.

I allow myself to trust in love.

Love surrounds me, and I give and receive it with ease.

I release all jealousy and possessiveness.

I acknowledge my connectedness with all human beings.

I accept my vulnerability.

I accept my interdependence.

I release all resentment, negativity, and remorse.

I forgive and move forward.

I am whole.

I release the need to control people, places, and things.

I love my job.

I love my family.

I love my partner.

I love my children.

I love my animals.

I love my life.

I focus on what I have in common with others.

The more love I give, the more I receive.

I reclaim my freedom to love.

Chapter 12

HOPE

"Hope
Smiles from the threshold of the year to come,
Whispering "it will be happier."

—Alfred, Lord Tennyson

As you arrive at the end of your journey through this book, there is one last principle to embrace—Hope. Surrendering to hope requires a tremendous leap of faith. It means trusting the words of others, when those of us who are sober tell you that the best years of your life lay ahead of you. Somewhere in your heart you must trust a process that you can't quite understand yet. It takes time. But with a practical toolset of exercises, coping skills, and new knowledge, you can look forward to a future full of possibility and joy, not to mention freedom from the debilitating chains of addiction. As we have discussed in almost every chapter, our brains, bodies, minds, and spirits are incredibly resilient. No matter how long we have lived in darkness, we can step out into the light and learn to love the sunshine. We *can* rewire our brains, and we can do it quickly and easily. Thousands have taken this path before you and they have achieved a life beyond their wildest dreams. *Rewired* is a roadmap. You just need to take the first step down the road and you *will* succeed.

Above all, be gentle with yourself. Know that every one of us, regardless of our circumstances, struggles with fear, self-doubt, loneliness, alienation, and despair. Those emotions describe the human condition, not just the state of the addict upon entering recovery. Knowing that you are not alone is one of the most important concepts you can take away from this book.

Another thing to remember is that you don't have to wait for results. Like Dorothy clicking her magic shoes, you have had the innate power to create the life you desire and deserve all along. Now you are finally ready to own that power. Your new behavior starts today, and just as quickly, your brain will forge new pathways and patterns. In other words, practicing the principles in this book is like falling into a "good rut." Having an open mind, an open heart, and the willingness to take action is the key. Incomprehensible beauty and peace await when you treat yourself with kindness and compassion, allowing yourself to live a healthy life.

You need only believe in yourself as much as I do.

From the depths of my heart, I wish you the greatest experience of love and happiness it is possible to know.

—Erica

APPENDIX: FOR FRIENDS AND LOVED ONES OF ADDICTS

There are countless people out there who know someone struggling with addiction, dependent behaviors to substances, or who are suffering due to their habits, behaviors, or lifestyle. Over the years, I have had many family members, friends, spouses, co-workers, and various others ask me for advice on how to speak with their loved one, friend, or colleague. There are also times where someone may be questioning whether the person they care about has a problem or not.

I would like to answer some of these questions and provide some guidance for all the bystanders feeling the effects of these problematic behaviors.

What are the signs, red flags, and things to look for?
Changes in mood/mood swings, a preference for isolation, lying, hiding and keeping secrets, weight loss or gain, depression, bouts of anxiety, and other negative consequences—arrests, DUIs, fighting with people, and so on.

How do we speak or communicate our concern?
Always come from a place of empathy. Use kind words that demonstrate your compassion. For example:

"It seems that you aren't happy, and I know that you deserve to live a good life."

"I know it must be hard for you to be dealing with this. I am here for you, if you ever need anything. We can find you some help, a therapist/

counselor to speak with, a program, treatment center, or some alternative form of healing."

"I am proud of you for having the courage to ask for help. That takes great strength."

Should I act a certain way? Is "tough love" a good idea?
Always try to express hope, no matter how desperate the situation may seem. Also, try to remember that we can be loving even when we work to create boundaries. Try to be supportive yet strong in your resolve; show that you are concerned first and foremost for their well-being.

RESOURCES

There are so many wonderful resources out there for addicts, their family members, friends and co-workers of substance users and those dealing with hardship.

It is very difficult for family members to see their loved one disintegrate, become unhealthy, lose their spirit, and get taken advantage of. It is imperative that the addict get the support they need, become educated and learn a new set of tools for how to cope.

ORGANIZATIONS

Alcoholics Anonymous (AA) (aa.org)

Adult Children of Alcoholics (ACA) (adultchildren.org)

All Addictions Anonymous (alladdictionsanonymous.org)

Al-Anon.org (al-anon.org)
For family members of addicts.

Cocaine Anonymous (CA) (ca.org)

Crystal Meth Anonymous (CMA) (crystalmeth.org)

Dual Recovery Anonymous (UK) (dualrecoveryanonymous.org)
A 12-Step program for those with a dual diagnosis.

Food Addicts in Recovery Anonymous (FA) (foodaddicts.org)

Gamblers Anonymous (GA) (gamblersanonymous.org)

Narcotics Anonymous (NA) (na.org)

Nar-Anon (nar-anon.org)
For family members of addicts.

Nicotine Anonymous (nicotine-anonymous.org)

Marijuana Anonymous (marijuana-anonymous.org)

Methadone Anonymous (methadonesupport.org)

S-Anon (sanon.org)
For family members of sex addicts.

Sexaholics Anonymous (sa.org)

Sex and Love Addicts Anonymous (SLAA) (slaafws.org)

Smart Recovery (smartrecovery.org)

Women for Sobriety (WFS) (womenforsobriety.org)

XA Speakers (xa-speakers.org)
A collection of recordings from speaker meetings, conventions, and workshops of 12-Steps (12step.org) resources for all 12-Step programs. It contains an in-depth discussion and forum on the 12 steps.

Find Treatment Centers in the USA

Recovery.org
A list of addiction recovery services and treatment centers around the world.

ONLINE SELF-HELP FORUMS

AA Intergroup (aa-intergroup.org)

Addiction Recovery Guide (addictionrecoveryguide.org)

Addiction Survivors (addictionsurvivors.org)

NA Chat (na-chat.com)

Soberistas (soberistas.com)

Support Groups (supportgroups.com)
Covering a wide range of issues, including addiction, depression, anxiety, and suicide.

12-Step Forums (12stepforums.net)

TREATMENT LOCATORS

Treatment Locator for the US
Substance Abuse Treatment Facility Locator
(findtreatment.samhsa.gov)
A database of drug and alcohol treatment programs in the U.S.

Treatment Locators for Ontario
Drug and Alcohol Helpline (*drugandalcoholhelpline.ca*)

Mental Health Helpline (*mentalhealthhelpline.ca*)
Free information and referral services for Ontario that are available to both the public and health professionals.

ABOUT THE AUTHOR

Erica **Spiegelman** is a consultant, author, counselor and speaker who has made an indelible mark in the field of addiction recovery. She has founded a multi-media health and wellness platform, providing consulting and counseling solutions for clients by providing them with tools on how to reach emotional, mental and physical freedom. She holds a Bachelor's degree in Literature from the University of Arizona and a degree as a California State Certified Drug and Alcohol Counselor (CADAC-II) from University of California, Los Angeles. Erica works with several treatment centers in California, including the Living Rebos Treatment Center, Klean Treatment Center, and Passages Malibu. She is a regular contributor to online health outlets, writes for Maria Shriver, and often co-hosts a weekly radio show Klean Radio on Sirius XM.

ALSO BY ERICA SPIEGELMAN

ISBN 978-1-57826-684-5

ISBN 978-1-57826-731-6

Available at www.hatherleighpress.com and wherever books are sold.